ONO

Options Not Obligations

Enrich Your Personal Life,
by Rethinking Your Financial Life

MARC WARNKE

New York

ONO

Options Not Obligations

ISBN 978-1-60037-601-6
Library of Congress Control Number: 2009901323

MORGAN · JAMES
THE ENTREPRENEURIAL PUBLISHER

Morgan James Publishing, LLC
1225 Franklin Ave., STE 325
Garden City, NY 11530-1693
Toll Free 800-485-4943
www.MorganJamesPublishing.com

In an effort to support local communities, raise awareness and funds, Morgan James Publishing donates one percent of all book sales for the life of each book to Habitat for Humanity. Get involved today, visit **www.HelpHabitatForHumanity.org**.

What Others are Saying About ONO

I moved out of the city to enjoy the outdoors and my family but I have not really taken the time to do that because I have been so busy with my business. ONO has helped to remind me of the things in life that I have been overlooking. In turn, I have reevaluated both my business and personal goals in life.

~Beau Value, Owner/CEO, Everest Construction

"ONO" has not only inspired me to think differently, but more importantly made me want to act differently. The book has helped kick me out of the rut of my traditional 9 to 5 job and encouraged me to search for alternatives that will allow me to have the option to spend time with my family as we grow, rather than the obligations that require me to sit at a desk. In five years, I want to be able to play golf on Tuesday and hang out with my family all summer long — without the worry that by doing so, I won't make next month's mortgage. As Marc would say, "that will be delicious."

~Travis Franklin, Business Executive

I only wish I had read Marc's book 35 years ago. This book is not your typical self-help book. ONO helps you understand how applying a little discipline to your life can drastically change your lifestyle and your career to give yourself the inner peace that ONO offers. I'm buying fifty copies to give to my friends and family members.

~Doak Worley, Business Owner/Sales Specialist

I wish I could make this mandatory reading for everyone in our company. A GREAT read that simplifies how to obtain your life's purpose & dreams.

~Joe LaVeque, CEO, Frist American Realty and Mortgage

Too often common sense is mislabeled as just a cliché. Marc takes 1000-year-old principles and applies them to our modern (and very busy) lives to help us remember what really matters. Like the words of our grandfathers, Marc's words will stick in your soul.

~Justin Foster, CEO, Tricycle Consultants

It is great to see a business book that touches on important topics such as spending, family & faith. I found the tone of the book to be informative, and not "lecturing" or "cramming it down your throat" & that was great.

~Dale Lenz, Co-Founder of Two Lane Tech, Inc.

There are tons of people just begging for direction on how to improve their life and feel better about their relationships...this book without doubt will inspire them to do something about the pain and move into action!

~Tom Steelman, Owner, Helmstar Group

Dedication

This book is dedicated to my wife Sue, my sons Jaken and Tucker, and to God for trusting me with the duty of being the man in their life.

Acknowledgements

Sue Warnke - Thanks to my wife who supports me unconditionally and is the wind in my family's sails.

Jaken Warnke - He has been inspirational in the content of this book and has made me a better man.

Tucker Warnke - My new little guy, bringing me gifts every day.

Carla Arnold - My lead in-house editor and irreplaceable cheerleader.

Boe Benefield - One of the unsung heroes in the development and production of this book and my indispensible personal assistant.

Peggy Jordan - My lead content editor and the reason this book isn't 400 pages too long. Her ability to organize and write content was simply invaluable. She was willing to become personally involved in the project and definitely brought her heart and soul to it.

Robin Tait - She reviewed an early draft and helped me to see a perspective that gave the book new clarity.

Kab Benefield - He is a spiritual mentor for me. His belief in me, and in this cause, has been critical to the energy behind this project.

Beau and Carrie Value - The couple who were instrumental in helping me discover ONO in my own life.

Bob Farewell - He has been a blessing in my life both spiritually and as a role model in parenting.

Chris Verhaegh - The long-term business mentor who cheered me along as I grew.

Justin Foster - Justin has been a steady reflector to me throughout the marketing of this book. His intellect has been priceless.

Glenn Alves - He has been a good friend and partner in the promotion of the total project.

Maryanna Young – She has helped me bridge the gap between being an author and business owner. Can't thank her enough for her stable presence in building ONO.

Chris Breshears – Chris has been super helpful in bringing this non-techie author up to speed with our online endeavors.

Sam Swenson – He has been extremely helpful in establishing our online efforts.

Kenny Lauer - Kenny was the person who inspired me to write this book. ONO would not be here without his encouragement and belief in me.

Virgil Tanner - He is one of my most supportive, encouraging inner-circle business partners. He has been one of my best examples of living with purpose.

Travis Franklin - He was my first fan and has become a close friend. Travis was the first to validate this book's power to affect real change.

Mark Steisel - His help in evaluating a near-finished copy took us closer to our goal of excellence. He was very helpful, encouraging, and competent in his evaluation and I would recommend him to anyone in the writing world.

Andris and Christy Lannon - This couple has supported me throughout in expanding intellectual concepts, and I especially appreciate Christy's help with web site photography.

Cory and Coletti Glauner—Their support has helped make this book the best it could be. Cory has been selfless in the support he has given.

Marilyn Watts - She was a key player in my emotional development and I can't thank her enough for her help in making me the man I am today.

Aaron Chandler - He is a friend and a fellow Family First Entrepreneur who has been there for me throughout this project by giving insight and by reading early copies more than once.

Tom Steelman – He has given support spiritually, emotionally, and financially.

The following list of people are friends and acquaintances that read early copies of ONO and gave me invaluable advice on how to make it better. Thanks to all of you.

- Curtis Ghelfi
- Bart Hendricks
- Betsy Davis
- Doak Worley
- Elijah Rich
- Joe LaVaque
- Toby Bingham
- Mark Reynolds
- Mike White
- Ivan Enochson

These are mentors in my life that I would like to thank. Many of their words are in this book.

- Barry Brahm
- Troy Hein
- Orville Thompson
- Dave Hurley
- Jim Boyd
- Kemo Sundquist
- Terry Mann
- Clive Johnston

There are several authors and speakers who have influenced me in profound ways. Here are a few of the major ones.

- Marc Victor Hansen
- Anthony Robbins
- Stephen Covey
- Zig Ziglar

Contents

Introduction

This is not just a book about making money. It will help you become financially successful, but it does not stop there. The goal is to help you succeed in all areas in your life. When you combine financial and personal success, you will be in a better position to fulfill your intended purpose here on earth.

I believe in loving the people in my life more than any other thing. ONO: *Options not Obligations* is the story of how I discovered this simple truth. It took me awhile; in fact, it was not until I held my first child in my arms that I realized that all my wealth, all my possessions, even my life itself, would never mean as much to me as my wife and children. So, I evolved from an entrepreneur into a Family First Entrepreneur. It was that simple.

Deathbed Epiphany

Sam Walton's deathbed epiphany story is one of the high-power examples of what I think are the truly important things in life. Walton, the founder and creator of Wal-Mart, muttered the words, "I blew it," on his deathbed. This was a man who contended for the title of richest man in the world, and these were his last words.

Sam Walton started the largest retail chain in America from the ground up. He had true financial wealth. He could buy anything he wanted, anytime he wanted. So, what did he mean when he said that he blew it? What could he have possibly done wrong?

Walton was referring to the fact that he regretted sacrificing too much of his time doing business, making money, and gaining power. He realized that it would have been better to spend that time with the people who were important in his life, the people who were gathered around his deathbed. Though it did not come until the end of his life, Sam Walton, an American business icon, finally realized the importance of the really juicy things in life—giving of yourself, putting your family first, building solid relationships, and helping others during your journey.

My Reaction

When I read Walton's last words, I was overcome with two emotions. The first was sadness. It is very sad that a man who accomplished so much in the business world, a man so highly respected, was personally and emotionally unfulfilled.

The second and stronger feeling that this story brought to me was motivation. I vowed never to let the tower of success cast a shadow over the most important thing in my life: my family. Our friends, our families, and most importantly, our children all spell love, "T-I-M-E." I have learned to prioritize my time. I always keep my family at the top of the list.

I am also a spiritual man, and I believe there is a divine plan for my life. I believe all things happen for a reason and valuable lessons are there for those who seek them out. I want to teach you to be a seeker. I want to inspire you to find your "Higher Purpose" here on earth and to remain on the lookout for ways to achieve it. That's where the inspiration to write this book began.

About Me

I said earlier that this is not *just* a book about making money. But, what you're about to read in these pages will give you the tools to create abundant wealth. I know the principles of ONO will work for you because I've used them successfully throughout my life.

- I have earned at least $200,000 a year entrepreneurially for the past 10 years.

- I made $1.5 million—in one year—when I was 35.

- I have never worked more than 9 months a year in my adult life.

- I have the luxury of employing a full-time personal assistant.

- Shortly after my first son was born, I was able to "retire" to savor every moment of being a hands-on dad.

- I have not needed to look for a regular job since I left college.

- I have the time and money to indulge my passions—spending time with the people I love, enjoying the outdoors, and traveling the world.

While all these things about me are true, this is not a book about me. This is a book about the idea of building wealth entrepreneurially with the intent to make a difference in our communities and families. ONO is the secret to the financial freedom that will enable you to be a Family First Entrepreneur.

In this book, I will be introducing to you both a lifestyle and a path to follow that will allow money to create wealth and produce positive changes in your life. When we don't have fears about having enough money, we are free to focus on things greater than ourselves. We can devote energy to a Higher Purpose: spend a lot more time with our children, volunteer to do church work, help kids learn to read, donate time, effort or money to a favorite cause, or even shovel rhino poop at the zoo. Whatever it is, we all have some burning desire to do good deeds.

My goal is to make that decision possible for you. This book, along with my goal to launch two moral, spiritual, and prepared sons into the world, is my current "pay it forward" attempt. I want you to find that same motivation and passion. I believe you will benefit from and love what I have written, and I can't wait to share it with you.

One: ONO, a Delicious Place

*What if you had many options about how to spend your time
and you had plenty of money to do
whatever you wanted?*

Ono is a Hawaiian adjective that means "delicious," in terms of food. My mom grew up in Hawaii in the fifties and sixties on the outer islands where things were still pretty *Hawaiian*. There weren't many tourists—everybody was "family"—there was lots of sun, lots of fun, and lots of great, great food. If you've ever been to Hawaii, or if you've ever had a chance to hang around with Hawaiian people, you know that they LOVE good food. That's what a luau is all about: ono food, good fun, and good people.

So, you ask, what does "good," as in "delicious," have to do with a success strategy? Well, how would you like to be at a place in your life where you could spend your time doing whatever you wanted?

- What if you didn't have to worry about making enough money to support your family or to meet your other obligations?

- What if money, or the lack of it, was no longer making decisions for you?

- What if that time came sooner rather than later?

- What if you had plenty of options about how to spend your time and plenty of money to do whatever you wanted?

1

- What if you had **O**ptions, **N**ot **O**bligations? That not only spells ONO, it is ONO.

What Are Obligations?

Obligations are all the things in your life that require action, time, money, or any combination of the three. There are obligations you impose on yourself like working out, going to church, or visiting grandma. There are financial obligations: mortgage or rent, insurance, utilities, childcare, and all the other bills you work so hard to pay. You have other obligations, too, like going to work, cooking meals, doing housework, and taking care of your possessions.

Dissect one week of your life. If you think about what you do and where you spend your money during one week, you will probably get a good sense of what your obligations are. Now think about how much of that time is spent doing what you choose to do, what you want to do, as opposed to what you are obligated to do. Added together, you will probably see that our obligations take up most of our time and most of our money.

What About Options?

Let's switch perspectives. Imagine that you had enough money to do what you really wanted. Imagine yourself with options. Options could be things like spending more time raising your children, being a better spouse, going fishing on a weekday, getting fit, growing a garden, or pursuing a lifelong dream. No matter what your ambition is, obligations can hold you back from fulfilling it. If you had enough, or more than enough money, wouldn't your obligations then become options? You could choose how to spend your time.

Better yet, what if you could make money:

- if you wanted;
- when you wanted;
- the way you wanted;
- as much or as little as you wanted?

You can have Options Not Obligations at any income level, but at the lowest levels you may have to live in a cardboard box and ride a bike. If you limit your lifestyle enough, almost anyone can have ONO, but most people want more than a box and a bike. That's the cool part—you get to choose. I want you to realize that the road to ONO does involve sacrifice, but my hope is that if you adhere to sound principles, you won't have to sacrifice too much.

The Road to ONO

How do you get to that place I call ONO, that place in your life where you're free to take advantage of the finer things in life without the obstacle of obligations standing in your way? It takes money. You need enough money to be free of the demands it makes on your time.

If you were at a place of choice where you could choose the way you spend your time, where money was not making decisions for you, if you were at a place of Options, not Obligations, wouldn't that be delicious? Yep, I thought so.

Where ONO Came From

I'm not a writer. I'm a talker—a public speaker, in fact. I'm also a reader, a voracious one, but not a writer. This is not a disclaimer; it is an explanation of how this book came to be. It came from conversations.

The idea for the title of the book was born during a conversation with a friend about being in a perfect position in my life. I had a slew of options and was unrestricted by any financial obligations.

The book's words, sentences, paragraphs, and chapters grew and matured, were hashed and rehashed, were clarified and solidified, in conversations. I did what I do well; I talked. I made appointments with colleagues and friends, held deliberate and purposeful conversations with them, and then I recorded the conversations.

The content? I've been carrying parts of it around inside me since I was a boy. The rest is the result of a fifteen-year quest to learn how to be a success in life, not only a success in business, but also a success as a man, in relationships and in spirituality.

Building the content of ONO is the story of building my life. You see, I've been very fortunate; two big factors in my life, both of which some people might consider stumbling blocks, have been critical stepping-stones in my path to success. They determine the way I acquire information and the way I look at it.

Dyslexia

The first is that I have a diagnosed learning disability. I am dyslexic. It caused me quite a bit of grief in school but has been a blessing in other parts of my life because when I distill information for myself, I cut to the chase. I discard the irrelevant and the unnecessary and find the gems that work for me. I make complex concepts simple, understandable, and workable. I have read hundreds of books on all sorts of topics, listened to hundreds of tapes and CDs, and talked to hundreds of people. I broke down the information I gained from them so that I could digest it and use it.

My disability has been a God-given gift. It allowed me to create easy-to-understand systems for myself: business systems, life and marriage systems, and belief systems. Those systems make up the content of this book. They reflect fifteen years of my life, years I spent gleaning, distilling, and implementing them.

Alcoholism

I encountered the second stepping-stone when I was in my teens. I became an adolescent alcoholic. When I became sober at age twenty-two, I was blessed with the opportunity to "remake" myself. I was able to choose new friends, set goals, learn to be a good man, and live my life with purpose and with joy.

In the "remaking of Marc," I became very aggressive in my mission to learn from the wisdom of others. I looked for people who seemed to be doing it right, and I found out what they were doing and how. I tried their methods and adapted the ones that worked for me to build my own financial, personal, and spiritual success.

As a result, this book is a distillation of the ideas I acquired from many sources. I intend to present them to you as methodologies of thought, not action.

A New Way of Thinking

I need to be very clear about this from the outset. This book was not written to teach you "how to do," but rather to teach you a much more valuable tool, "how to think." Let me give you two examples of what I mean.

First, I am a firm believer in *mentors*. They are an invaluable source of information and assistance. Mentors have had a huge impact on my life; they have taught me some useful tactics and strategies. But, more important than the tactics and strategies were the insights I gained by paying attention to the reasons behind what my mentors did. It was important to me to learn not only why successful people did what they did, but also *how they thought* about each situation.

Learning how to think in business was by far the most valuable lesson I ever learned as an entrepreneur because no two situations are ever the same. I learned to wrap a thinking style around my decisions that took into account all the variables. You will encounter many similar situations, but the variables will be unique to you and your life. My goal is to give you important background information that will help you make better decisions in your business dealings no matter what the variables are.

Second, I am also a firm believer in *reading* for information. There are millions of entrepreneurial opportunities available to you, and all of them have been dealt with in great detail in hundreds of how-to books. Bookstores are loaded with topics like "How to Invest in Real Estate," "How to Start Your Own Business," "How to Make Money in the Stock Market," and the list goes on and on.

I have gleaned a lot of useful information from books like these but found that one key element was missing from most of them, which is *how to think about the process*. I had to read between the lines to find the insights I was looking for. Now I am passing those insights on to you. I don't want to merely teach you how to fish, I also want to teach you how successful fishermen think, which is much more valuable.

ONO, a Delicious Place

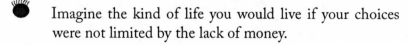 Imagine the kind of life you would live if your choices were not limited by the lack of money.

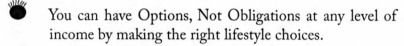 You can have Options, Not Obligations at any level of income by making the right lifestyle choices.

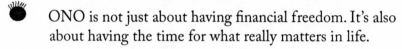 ONO is not just about having financial freedom. It's also about having the time for what really matters in life.

Two: The Family First Entrepreneur

Time with the family takes priority over buying that Ferrari.

In the introduction, I mentioned that I was on the path to being a Family First Entrepreneur. These three words came from a brainstorming session I had while on a road trip. I was trying to come up with a "simple idea" that cut to the marrow of how I see myself as a person. When I voiced the words, "Family First Entrepreneur," I realized I had created a statement that was simple enough and powerful enough to create a movement.

A Family First Entrepreneur is someone with an entrepreneurial mindset who keeps his or her family first.

As we look more deeply into this definition, we must acknowledge that when business people put their families first, those two elements—business and family—affect one another in profound ways. For example, when I want time with my kids, that choice relates to and has a direct effect on the time I spend on business and other endeavors.

Family First Entrepreneurs make business choices based on the potential impact they will have on their families first, and on business profitability second.

People who align with this principle realize that their families' ability to function properly also affects their businesses. There is nothing like family trauma to make a day at work both unbearable and unproductive. They realize they need a healthy marriage and family life to be their best while producing a living. At the same time, making a good living is part of keeping your family healthy and safe, so a successful business is one of the best gifts you can give to the people who depend on you. Family First Entrepreneurs need a healthy work-life balance, because the two are so interconnected.

Lastly, Family First Entrepreneurs have an attitude about wealth creation that puts the goal of building wealth for the enhancement of their family first, and for material possessions second.

Whether you're an empty nester, a single person, or have chosen not to have children, you still have a "family." If you are someone who puts your family first, who wants work-life balance, and who would enjoy creating wealth entrepreneurially, I welcome you.

The Family First Entrepreneur

- When you put your family first, the two elements—business and family—affect each other in profound ways.

- Entrepreneurs need a healthy marriage and family life to be at their best while producing a living.

- Becoming a successful entrepreneur is an honorable way to support and care for your family.

Three: Call to Action

When the pain is greater than the fear, you will move.

I believe many Americans have developed a huge tolerance for what I define as the eight-to-five pain. Most of us learn to deal with it, and even scarier, to accept it in our everyday lives. What is pain? Pain is being forced to go to a job that drains us every single day, 50 weeks a year. Pain is barely making enough money to provide for our families' basic needs. Pain is not being able to spend quality time with our children, or doing what we need or want to do to relax and enjoy life because that time is limited by our occupations.

This pain has become the norm. Most people trudge through life bearing it because they believe there is no other option.

It's Your Choice

The truth is you don't have to live with this pain. Many people have discovered this. They have taken control of their lives and have decided to make a difference for themselves and their families. They were willing to do whatever it took, even if it meant taking risks and making a huge leap of faith in order to free themselves.

Unfortunately, the number of people who have taken action to free themselves from pain is minuscule compared to those still pinned down by the burden of their obligations. The funny thing is that the number of people aware of the opportunity to live differently is gigantic. *So,* why don't more people try it? Because the thing holding them back is a core-level emotion. We have all battled it our entire lives. It is called fear.

Imagine a large rushing river. On one side of the river are people in a constant struggle with pain, less than 90 days from bankruptcy, stuck in the drudgery of living as slaves to their obligations, and wishing they could break free.

On the other side of the river are those people living the ONO lifestyle. They have the time and ability to do what they want when they want.

The people weighed down by obligations see what those on the other side have, and they long to join them, but they can't see past the challenge of crossing the river. They see the rapids, the deep water, and fear causes them to freeze. They are stuck. They doubt their abilities and have no intention of stepping outside their comfort zones and taking risks.

If this sounds like you, I'm challenging you to begin looking at life in a new way. If you have no desire to change, I have no ability to help you.

Systems

If you're still reading, great! That means you believe there is a better way to live, and you're willing to face your fears to seek it out. I believe that one of the *biggest fears* about the idea of creating options instead of obligations is the fear of being responsible for every aspect of your own life. It's only natural. We have been raised to rely on others. We have all been part of some system, most of us several systems, since we were born. We were in a family system, then an educational system, and many of us have been part of a religious system as well. Most of us are currently in a work system. We work day after day, all year long.

We can all relate to this because we have all experienced it. We have been taught that the way to get by in any system is to work hard and to fit in. We follow the rules and hope our hard work and sacrifice will keep us moving from the bottom to the top.

There are other ways to get us where we want to go. Some of us have created our own systems, and started at the top rather than the bottom.

What an exciting idea! It excites most people…until they begin thinking about the logistics of making that idea a reality and they think they have to do it all at once.

Hurdles

The largest stumbling block to crossing that river is that people are overwhelmed by all the details involved in creating their own entrepreneurial venture. They look at every aspect all at once. They see it as a huge task with many unknown variables, which increases the risk factor and therefore increases their fear. That river is daunting, and many people doubt their ability to reach the other side even before they get their feet wet.

Let me remind you, your journey across that river starts with an idea for finding new financial opportunities. That does not necessarily mean starting a new business. *An entrepreneurial venture is anything that will create additional income.* It does not have to be very big at first.

No matter how big or small the venture is, when people look at the entire river, they doubt themselves and feel fear. They lose themselves, their perspective, their vision of the bigger picture. Those emotions are part of human nature. Because activity is scary, they choose inactivity. Inactivity takes us nowhere. I guarantee it. There are very few guarantees in life but this is one: do nothing, get nothing. Inactivity is fenced in by fear.

Take Control

The first key step to taking control is to break out of that stagnant emotion. When the pain is greater than the fear, you will move. Though fear may be doing everything it can to keep you stuck, it can be overcome.

Think about all of the pain you and your family have had to go through. Now, imagine yourself pain and obligation-free for the rest of your life. Imagine how it looks, sounds, feels, even tastes. If you can imagine it, even briefly, then you are open to the possibility of moving toward ONO. A mindset open to the idea of taking action is all it takes.

What I have experienced, both in my own life and through talking with other successful individuals, is that for many of us it takes a transition moment, a shocking event or realization to completely change our mindset from fear to action. Family trauma, a divorce, a death, an inspirational conversation, or even a book can be the catalyst for change.

Perhaps you're experiencing that transition moment. For whatever reason, you are on your way to making a change in your life, but you can't dive in without making some preparations first. Don't be in a hurry to rush into anything. The chapters that follow will help you strategically plan your course across the river, show you where to find the shallow spots and the stepping-stones to make the crossing easier.

Beyond Money

The title of the book, "ONO: Options, Not Obligations," came out of a conversation with one of my favorite business partners, Virgil Tanner. I had just closed a big deal. I had just swung for the fence, connected with the ball, and knocked one out of the park. As he already knew, this had not happened by accident.

At the time, my wife Sue and I had been on the road for three years, running our business from an RV. The business was supporting us well, but our home on the road was far from comfortable. It had been bearable when it was just the two of us, but after our son, Jaken was born, I knew that even though the money was great, the traveling life was not for me anymore. I wanted more time to be a father. We had traveled 254 days during the previous year on business, and traveled nine months of that year with an infant. It was craziness. The money was not worth the sacrifices we had been making.

The good news was, during those three years, because we made good money and lived frugally, we had achieved two important goals: we had paid off all our debts and accumulated a good-sized investment account. (I call it my ONO account. You'll hear more about that later.) Up until then, all my business ventures had been small-scale, but when Jaken was born, I made the decision to take on a big project. My swing-for-the-fence project was a multimillion-dollar resort spec house. I knew if this deal went through, it would be my chance to get out, to break us free.

The Breakthrough

Our hopes were realized. We sold the property and put almost a million dollars in the bank. That was my break loose point. That's where I could say, "Okay, now I have choices about doing what I want to do. I can *choose* how I make a living because I have a massive buffer behind me."

Thanks to the money in the bank, I was in a position to free myself from the burnout of all that traveling. I said, "You know what Virgil? The neatest part about having this money in the bank is that I now have created a situation for myself where **I have options as opposed to obligations.**"

Making money is great, but this book is about more than that; it's about being free to dream. It's about having enough money to break loose, to fulfill our duties to our families, our fellow man, and ourselves. It is about enjoying our lives because we have plenty of money to do so. I want to help you make money, as much money as you want, but I also want to help you get *beyond money*, to what life is truly all about.

Measuring Success

You don't need a lot of money to be at ONO. You can have Options, not Obligations making $40,000 a year or $400,000 a year. I've seen people who have reached ONO at $40,000 and I've seen people who don't have ONO at $400,000 a year.

It's not about the money. It's about not having the pursuit of money interfere with the pursuit of life. It's about where you are now and where you want to be. That's what's so exciting. Everybody can get to ONO, and you can start from where you are right now.

Call to Action

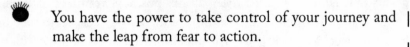 You have the power to take control of your journey and make the leap from fear to action.

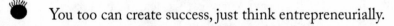 You too can create success, just think entrepreneurially.

Everybody can get to ONO, and you can start from where you are right now.

Four: Getting to That Place Called ONO

What if you could pick out everything you really wanted instead of only what you could afford?

I'd be willing to bet that when you go into a restaurant and look at the menu, you read it right to left. You look at the prices on the right-hand side, and then look to the left and make your selection based on which items are in your price range. I know about this because I've done it, too.

The Menu of Life

Being at a place in your life where price was not a factor would make it so much easier. What if you covered up the prices and made your choice? You'd get what you really wanted, wouldn't you? That's ONO. It is where you have many options, and where money has no influence on your decision-making.

If you could read the Menu of Life in the same way, wouldn't that be perfectly delicious? You could and would make choices based on what you *really* wanted, rather than on what you could afford. If you wanted to live differently, maybe move to a more upscale neighborhood, you would, and there would be nothing to stop you. If you wanted to be a full-time parent, maybe even home school your kids or send them to a different school, you could choose those options without even considering the cost. You would not have to chase money all the time. You could spend your time doing the finer things, the things money cannot buy, because you wouldn't have to worry about making money.

The ONO Menu of Life has no price restraints. It includes the truly juicy parts of life, the extra things most of us think we may never get the chance to enjoy, like dessert. Being at ONO means we have the opportunity to focus on the benefits of having wealth as opposed to having to spend all our time pursuing that wealth.

Your Higher Purpose

In order to reach the position of being able to read the Menu of Life from left to right, you have to start somewhere. *Begin at the end.*

The path to ONO begins with being **result-focused**. Sketch out your path to the place of Options, Not Obligations, and picture yourself at the end of that path.

Put yourself in a position of casting aside the mental block that not having enough money places on your creative thinking. What would you do with your life if you had all the money you needed? That goal is what I call your Higher Purpose. I believe every one of us has an idea of what we would do with our time and our money if we had an abundance of both.

For each of us, that Higher Purpose is greater than we are. It is what we dream of doing. For most people, it is in the form of a gift or a way of giving back. Maybe your Higher Purpose is to help AIDS victims in Africa, or donate a large sum of money to a charity organization. Maybe it's to start a learning group, to volunteer time at a local hospital, or to take better care of your family. Maybe it's to play with your kids more or go back to school. No matter what they are, we all have dreams and aspirations.

My Higher Purpose is threefold. I want to be a better husband, a hands-on father, and, ever since the conversation I had with Virgil, I also want to teach others how they can get their families to ONO.

That's my goal. Now, the question is, "What is *your* Higher Purpose? We will draw the path that leads to it next.

Begin at the End

Higher Purposes require time. However, time is something you have to buy. So how are you going to buy that time? How will you create enough time in your daily life to help you move toward fulfilling your Higher Purpose?

Step One: Your Epitaph

The first step is to figure out what you want your future life to look like. Evaluate where your life is headed now and compare that to your ideal lifestyle. Decide how you can fulfill your potential and leave your mark here on earth. If having to make money were not a part of the equation, what would you do to leave your legacy?

Figuring out that first step is not as tough as it sounds. I was at this exact moment fifteen years ago. I knew I wanted to be a success in business, and I was looking for a plan. I happened to pick up *Seven Habits of Highly Effective People* by Stephen Covey, which soon became one of my all-time favorite books. One of Covey's suggestions was to look at your goal and then plan steps to get there. He spoke about it in terms of *beginning at the end*. But how do you look at the end when you're talking about your life?

Covey introduced the idea of imagining what you would want to be said about you when you die. You might start as I did by writing an epitaph that might go on a headstone. For example, "Devoted Son, Loving Father, He Will Be Missed."

Step Two: Your Eulogy

Next, go deeper than that. Really think about what you want to accomplish in your life and write your own eulogy. Write a script that you would want to be read aloud at your funeral. What kind of person were you? Who and what were most important in your life? On what things, large and small, did you leave your mark? By the way, your eulogy would probably never mention your net worth.

Writing my own eulogy was one of the most humbling and inspiring tasks I have ever undertaken. I used it to figure out my three-fold Higher Purpose. It was at that point that I realized that money had to be there before I could make those things happen. My goal then became to reach the point where I had more money than I would ever need, so that I would have options about how I spent my money, and more importantly, how I spent my time.

So, write your eulogy. Once that is finished, the intentional journey begins. **Once you look at what you want to accomplish in your life, you will know your Higher Purpose.** This is your goal. Write it down and keep it handy; it will make it so much easier.

~ *Opportunity for Reflection* ~
Write your Eulogy.

_____

_____

_____

_____

_____

_____

_____

_____

Step Three: Your Higher Purpose

For every major decision, ask yourself, "Will this choice get me closer to my Higher Purpose?" This thought process will keep you from going off on tangents that do not serve your goals. In business, there are so many opportunities to get off track. In my own life, defining my Higher Purpose, IN WRITING, is what has kept me on track and helped me define the step-by-step processes that would take me there. So, plan for your future by starting at your Higher Purpose and work backward. Begin with your ultimate goal, and plan the way to get from your current situation to your Higher Purpose.

Seek Inspiration Regularly

Defining your Higher Purpose will give you a foundation and a source of inspiration and motivation, but you can't stop there. You must build on that foundation by looking for inspiration in your everyday life. Each person is inspired by different things and it is your job to find out what inspires you. It is so easy to get emotionally flattened by the steamroller of life and become weary of spirit. You need to be prepared for those "flat" times. Your strategic plan to get to ONO must include provisions for motivation and inspiration. Just as we must nourish our bodies, we must also nourish our spirits and our emotional selves. If we don't, when we get discouraged, we will not be as effective as we could and should be.

Inspiration can be found in so many areas of our lives: conversations with others, spending time with loved ones, creating or appreciating art, listening to religious sermons, going to seminars, or spending quiet time by ourselves. We all find inspiration in different ways.

When I need a lift, I watch a movie. I love watching true stories about someone who lets nothing stand in the way of his or her dreams. One of my all-time favorites is "Rudy." Stories like this remind me that anyone can accomplish anything with enough will and determination.

Any time I am feeling down and unmotivated, I pop in one of these movies and get an inspirational recharge. It is so important to find out what inspires you and seek those things out. They will help you to keep your Higher Purpose in mind and keep you moving forward effectively toward your goal.

Getting to That Place Called ONO

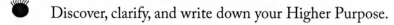 Discover, clarify, and write down your Higher Purpose.

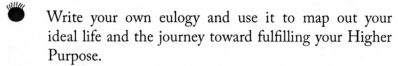 Write your own eulogy and use it to map out your ideal life and the journey toward fulfilling your Higher Purpose.

Find sources of inspiration you can turn to on a regular basis to keep yourself motivated. Visit my blog at www. MarcWarnke.com for some ideas and examples.

Five: Spirituality in Business

I am only in control of two things: my choices and my behaviors.

Spirituality is a touchy subject because so many of us, in one way or another, have been "spiritually abused" at some point in our lives. What I mean by that is that many of us have been shunned, or threatened, or have had religion shoved down our throats. I can relate. Because of that, I want to be clear that I have no personal stake in trying to get you to think the way I do spiritually. My intention is to tell you about how my spirituality has kept me serene and kept me learning while I had fun in business. It's not a prescription; it is merely one person's story.

My spirituality came from being a recovering alcoholic. I got sober in 1992. I learned through Alcoholics Anonymous to call on a power greater than myself to overcome my addiction and get my life moving in the right direction. I chose to call my Higher Power, "God." I knew I needed God to help me do something I couldn't do for myself.

Here's a fact that may startle you: only twenty percent of alcoholics take part in the AA program and only two percent die sober. For me, understanding that I had to fully surrender to God's will made the difference between living and dying.

Control

A full surrender to God's will means giving up the illusion of being in control of one's own life. This was a complex thought for me to grasp. Like most recovering alcoholics, I had great difficulty telling the difference between things I could control and things I couldn't.

Aspects of the economy, business systems, and the natural laws of business are uncontrollable, unpredictable, and even whimsical. If I told you that your business life would to be all cream and roses, I'd be lying. Most of us are told how to do things throughout our entire lives. We are told that if we think like the masses and follow certain steps, we can control our results and guarantee success. Then we jump into the business world without learning how to think for ourselves. More often than not, we get our tails kicked once and run away from the business world never to return.

However, when a person learns how to think in business, especially how to think spiritually in business, he or she may get a tail kicking, but will have the tools and understanding to make peace with it, learn from it, and move on to the next evolution. By making peace with results, good or bad, and knowing God as a loving entity is giving us the opportunity to learn, we can take greater strides than those people who are still trying to control results.

I obtained a great piece of wisdom one day from an ex-heroin addict who had achieved long-term sobriety. He was a scary looking guy. Had I not known him, and had I seen him coming down the street, I would have crossed the road just to stay away from him. He was very rough on the outside, but as I found out, he was kind and wise on the inside. Had I judged this man by his appearance, I would have missed something very important.

The man told me, "I am only in control of a couple things, and those are my choices and behaviors; everything else is up to my Higher Power." I had read and heard that before but never realized how simple and powerful that statement actually was.

It stunned me to realize that all I needed to worry about was my own behavior. I had always understood that it was my responsibility to do the footwork, the due diligence, and then to implement the knowledge and wisdom I gained through the AA program, but up to that point I had also been trying to control the results. When I heard his words, I experienced a transitional moment, a life changing, "Aha." It suddenly became very clear to me that I really had no control over the results. They were in the hands of God, my Higher Power.

I found peace in finally realizing this. From that point onward, I worked very hard to do my own footwork in life, but leave the results up to God. I implemented this insight in my business life, my spiritual life and my personal life and developed strategies that have allowed me to be "sober" in those three aspects of my life and to maintain my serenity.

As a spiritual man, when I look at a business equation, I know that I'm responsible for putting up the money, making decisions, marketing, and sales. I have to put the infrastructure in place. I have to employ the right people. All of these different things come with building and maintaining a functional business.

I'm responsible for all of the prep work, but the results of that effort are out of my hands. I could do everything right and it could turn out wonderfully, but as life has reminded me several times, it could still turn out to be a train wreck. The key to success is not worrying about a potential train wreck, it's being prepared for, learning from, and moving on from either success or the train wreck, whichever happens. That's serenity.

Shame

The fact is, being invested in the results of a business venture *can* hurt you. When you think that you can control results, you open the door to poor business decisions, wasted time, energy and money. To make matters worse, if you haven't learned to let go and find serenity in both success and failure, you can be devastated by such defeats.

It's natural to be embarrassed when something doesn't go as planned, but holding onto shame and using it as an excuse to beat yourself up is counterproductive. When you feel shame, understand and accept what you're feeling, and then move on. Don't dwell on it. Learn from your mistakes and be thankful for having new wisdom that takes you to the next opportunity. Use this process to release the shame and move on toward success with serenity.

When you're locked up in shame, you can't see a way to move through it. So, the natural choice is to stop and not make another move. This is *not* the mindset of successful entrepreneurs. **Successful entrepreneurs look at failure as an opportunity to learn from mistakes.** They move forward with new information and a new plan.

My personal serenity is one of my most valuable assets. I couldn't pay enough for it. In fact, it is beyond any monetary value. I would give up every penny of the financial success I've ever had to keep my serenity. It gives me long-term security in my business ventures whether they are successful or not. It also prevents bringing negativity back home with me.

As a Family First Entrepreneur, I refuse to allow my ability to discern between what I can or can't control to affect the quality of my time with my children or my wife. A person in business who does not have serenity is, in my opinion, like a bucket with a hole in it. It doesn't matter how much you fill that bucket up, if it has a hole in the bottom, it will eventually be empty. Serenity in business keeps your bucket full and keeps you on track.

Be Moral and Ethical

A large part of spirituality in business is making sure that all of your actions fall within the parameters of the highest moral and ethical standards. When profitability gets in the way of ethics, it is only a matter of time before a business blows up and goes under. If you keep your moral and ethical standards high, you'll attract a long list of people waiting to do business with you because they know they can count on your integrity. That simple fact alone is worth a fortune.

AA taught me the importance of being "service minded." As an alcoholic, I had developed selfish and self-centered attitudes; it is the nature of the disease. As I found my spirituality, I learned to adopt the mindset of service in both my personal life and business life. Now I consider ways I can "under-promise and over-produce."

A business must be operated to provide service rather than personal fulfillment. If your first thought is, "How can I help?" and your second thought is, "How can I make a profit?" you're coming from the right place. A business based on substandard moral and ethical considerations will always reach a point of vulnerability, at which point it must change and grow. If it continues to be self-serving at the expense of its customers, it will collapse.

Developing a healthy spiritual life will not only affect your chances of succeeding in business, but also your ability to maintain serenity and balance, which is what I believe it's all about. The road to ONO is not always going to be easy.

Now, I'm a realist. I know there are businesspeople out there that do not have a relationship with a Higher Power, and I'm not invested in converting anyone to my point of view. But for any entrepreneur, accepting responsibility for our own choices and behaviors and giving up the illusion of being able to control the outcome of every venture makes good business sense.

Operating morally and ethically is not only the right approach; it's also the only way to stay in business long-term. Do your footwork, do your due diligence and then let go of the results. Let the chips fall where they may. Be serene, trust that you have done your part, and be thankful for the lessons.

Spirituality in Business

- You are only in control of your choices and behaviors, the results of those choices are out of your hands.

- Giving the results up to a Higher Power offers a sense of serenity in the workplace.

- When you fail, learn from your mistakes, let go of the results, and move on to the next opportunity.

- Uphold the highest moral and ethical standards.

Six: False Beliefs about Wealth

"It is not the creation of wealth that is wrong, but the love of money for its own sake."

~Margaret Thatcher

What is wealth anyway? How do you define it? As a Family First Entrepreneur, I define wealth as an environment where my relationships and life experiences can flourish. When I create wealth and couple it with an ONO mindset, I can accomplish things greater than myself and affect positive change in and outside of my circle of influence.

The pursuit of success and wealth starts long before you actually put a single penny into your pocket. The process begins when you make the decision to change, when you decide you want to become wealthy. You must tell yourself that you have what it takes and that you are going to be successful no matter what obstacles stand in the way. One of the first obstacles to overcome is letting go of negative stereotypes about wealthy people.

Most people have had little, if any, interaction with truly wealthy people. Their feelings about the wealthy are based on hearsay and assumptions. Unfortunately, it is human nature to look for flaws in others rather than point out good, especially if the "others" have what we desire. So, we develop a skewed perception of people, or groups of people that we really know nothing about, and that includes wealthy people.

My Misconceptions

Like so many others, I was raised with this stereotype. My mom felt that people became rich through sheer luck. They had either inherited their fortunes or struck it rich somehow. She believed that normal people could get ahead in life only if they worked hard. Therefore, the harder and longer you worked, the more money you could make, but to acquire great wealth, you needed a stroke of luck.

My dad, on the other hand, was of the opinion that wealthy people were bad people, and he influenced me to hold that same opinion. His father had struggled as a farmer in the Midwest, and, like so many children of the Great Depression, he developed bitter feelings about the rich. He passed his beliefs on to my dad, and my dad—without any personal experience to back them up—passed them on to me. So when I was young, I used to say, "I'm not prejudiced against any group of people except the rich."

My dad's feelings were only strengthened by what he saw on TV and read in newspapers. When stories about wealthy people hit the news, they're usually negative stories. Stories of wealthy people doing wonderful things, like Jimmy Carter's and Bill and Melinda Gates' efforts in Africa, receive little press. News coverage about people who gain success and then devote their time and money to others is far overshadowed by coverage of those on the opposite end of the spectrum.

Wealthy people are perceived as having the easy life, spending money frivolously while the rest of us slave away. Along with that, they are seen as self-centered and selfish. It is a common belief that they became rich by taking unfair advantage of others. Because of these negative images, many Americans, along with people all over the world, believe that you cannot be a wealthy person and still be a good person.

These misconceptions are why so many people do not pursue the path to success. They know that having more money will ease their financial burdens, but they think they will turn into the kind of people they have been taught to dislike and distrust. They fear that having money will change who they are, and that this change will be for the worse.

As I matured and began to form opinions and beliefs based on my own experience and research, my perception of wealth began to change. I longed to be financially secure, and more than that, I longed to be able to afford more free time. So, in order to learn more about financial security, I did the only thing I knew how to do—I put myself in situations where I had a chance to interact with wealthy individuals.

Through these interactions, I came to realize that they were kindhearted, hardworking and overall good people. I realized that very few people became rich by stepping on the backs of others. This was an eye-opening and inspirational realization. I also discovered that the ones who were "snotty-rich" were usually the imposters in the group. They were the ones that made a lot of money, but spent even more. They were buried in debt, only cared about keeping up with the Joneses, and they were doing it on borrowed money. They appeared rich on the surface, but were not truly wealthy.

True Wealth is Earned

Very few successful individuals were born with, lucked out, or stumbled upon their wealth. In most cases, people who win the lottery or come into money by some non-conventional method never actually establish a long-term lifestyle of wealth. In fact, studies show that most individuals who instantly go from very little money to great wealth soon fall back to their old way of life in a short amount of time.

A television program I watched recently featured a homeless street person who was given $100,000 in cash. They told him to do whatever he wanted with it, the only stipulation was that they got to film him and document what he did with his money. Long story short—six weeks, two new pickup trucks and some other ridiculous purchases later, he was completely out of money again. Why? Because he didn't have the necessary background to handle his new situation. He hadn't done the work that it took to earn the money. He had no point of reference for financial security, so when he instantly acquired it, he had no idea how to maintain it.

Wealth is a responsibility. People can get stymied by the process if they haven't done the footwork and don't understand the responsibility that comes with earning and keeping wealth.

Almost all the wealthy individuals I've known built their wealth from the ground up. They were not born with money, they did not win the lottery, nor did they have any innate knowledge or wisdom. They were like most people; they didn't even have seed money to help ease them through the wealth-building process. Each individual's journey to wealth had been an exploration, as opposed to a defined path. Their journeys were made up of multiple opportunities, successes, and failures. They combined hard work with will and determination, and in the end, they created their own path to success, and they developed a firm sense of pride and respect for what they earned.

On the other side of the coin, some wealthy people maintain strong core values and personal responsibility even though they did not have to earn their fortunes the hard way. I have an acquaintance that is a wonderful example of this. He was born into an extremely wealthy family and, unlike many other individuals in the same situation; he took on the wealth he was given with pride, a sense of gratitude, and responsibility. He was determined to learn, to work hard, and to earn and preserve a reputation as a respectable businessman.

Maintaining this mindset was probably not easy for him because he was given so much throughout his life. His family is worth over a billion dollars. He owns his own yacht with a full-time staff. He once told me that he did not pump his own gas until he was in his 40's. His personal staff takes care of his every need.

It would have been easy for this man to live out his life being waited on hand and foot. He could have spent every day on the beach sipping piña coladas if he had wanted to, but instead he learned to invest his money and, at the same time, to create opportunities for others. He has true respect for other people. He values everyone he comes across, no matter how much money that person has. He is warm and genuine. He spends time in the community. He is friendly and hugs everyone. He is a great family man; he loves and spends lots of time with his wife and kids. He does not let money get in the way of the most important things in his life. He is eternally grateful for the situation he has been given and does not take it for granted. He contradicts all popular beliefs that wealthy people are unkind and selfish.

Wealthy People are Frugal

Another common belief about people of wealth is that they are frivolous and careless with their money. While some are (and have gained a lot of media attention because of it), most are very cautious and conservative when it comes to spending.

Let me tell you about an experience that I had one day out on the golf course. I was playing Osprey Meadows at Tamarack Resort, a very prestigious course in central Idaho. I love playing high-end courses, not just because of the courses themselves, but also because of the people with whom I get to play. Most of them have found financial success in some way or another. Being paired with such people is my chance to interact with and learn from them.

I love the conversations. Good conversation is the only thing that keeps me sane on the golf course, because the game itself drives me nuts.

One day I was paired with a man I soon learned was worth millions. He was a real player, both in the business world and on the golf course. I felt a little intimidated. His vast business knowledge and accumulation of wealth far overshadowed my own. Not only that, I was an average golfer, and the way I was playing that day made it look like it was my very first time. I was spraying the ball all over the course. I couldn't hit the ball straight if my life depended on it. Not only was I looking like a hack; I was slowing this guy down.

He never looked frustrated or annoyed with me, but I began to feel a little embarrassed.

As we played on, I hit the ball into some very deep rough. I thought, "Oh no, here we go again." I knew there was a snowflake's chance in Hell that we would find the ball in the knee-high grass, but he walked over with me to the area where the ball had disappeared and began looking for it. At this stage in the game, I had no desire to stop and look for the ball. I was playing slow enough as it was. I looked for a good ten seconds, dropped another ball and hit it, but I noticed that my new friend was still looking for my ball. I told him not to worry about it. I didn't want him to waste his time trying to find my ball.

Ignoring my request, he picked up a ball he found, read me the label and asked if it was mine. I told him it wasn't. With a grin, he wiped off the ball and put it into his pocket. "What about this one?" He held up another ball. Again, it was not mine. He pocketed it as well. The idea of finding two new golf balls for his collection tickled him so much that he looked like he had just won the lottery. This was a guy who could buy more golf balls than he could count in his lifetime, but he acted as though this was his lucky day because he had found two used $1 golf balls.

He found a third, and then a fourth. Seeing that he was in no hurry to get back to the game, and because at that point I could have cared less if I ever hit another ball in my life, I joined in the fun. Because it was a Tuesday and no one else was behind us, there we were, two grown men on a course with greens fees of over $150, each of us with a considerable net worth, digging in the grass and dirt looking for used golf balls. We were like two kids in a candy store. Once our pockets could not hold any more golf balls and our hands and shoes were covered in mud, we decided to call it quits. It was one of the best finishes to one of the lousiest beginnings that I have ever had on a golf course.

Make Wealth Your Goal

Let go of your biases about wealth if you still have any. Then, develop a new belief system, one where you truly believe that:

- You CAN be wealthy,

- You DESERVE to be successful, and

- You WILL create abundance in your life.

WARNING! While MOST of the world's wealthy are good people, exceptions do exist. Do not let yourself become one of those exceptions. As you progress down your path to success, remember what it was like before you made the decision to change your life. Never take any opportunity for granted.

Though you may have financial wealth, you will never have true ONO wealth if you operate from a place of greed. Greed is a green-eyed monster, and once you let it in, it demands to be fed. When you let greed take over, you no longer have options, you are back to obligations. You become obligated to feed your greed and next thing you know, your entire life revolves around it.

While I'm on the be-a-good-person soapbox, there's one more reminder I want to give you. There will be many times as you move toward wealth when you will experience success because another person either gave you information or created an opportunity that opened a door for you. Be grateful for that opportunity and make it your goal to open doors for others every time you have the chance. Wealth is about so much more than having money. Wealth is about having abundance and, at the same time, creating abundance for others.

False Beliefs about Wealth

- Despite popular belief, most wealthy people are good people.

- Wealth is earned by working with others, not stepping on the backs of others.

- Truly wealthy people are always on the lookout for new ways to save or to make money rather than looking for ways to blow it.

- You too can be wealthy—all it takes is the right mindset.

Seven: Think Like an Entrepreneur

The greatest risk of all is never taking a risk.

Once again, I'm going to ask you to learn to think a little differently. It is time to get into the mindset of creating wealth for yourself. In order to get to ONO and to achieve your Higher Purpose, I want you to begin thinking like an ONO entrepreneur.

What is an entrepreneur, anyway? *Webster's Dictionary* defines it as, "Someone who seeks to capitalize on new and profitable endeavors or business, usually with considerable initiative and risk."

I find this definition almost comical. First of all, "considerable initiative" doesn't go far enough; it's missing a little heart and a little soul. Second, it's enough to scare most people away from taking on an entrepreneurial venture because of the emphasis on the word "risk."

Risk

Let's talk about risk. Most beginning entrepreneurs risk only their time as they build profitability. They then use those profits as reinvestment capital as they grow. Time is all they invest initially and then wisdom becomes the guide for capital and growth management as they move forward. Risk itself means nothing without knowing what is actually being risked.

Risks occur every single minute of every single hour of every single day of our lives. What do we do, consciously or unconsciously, to live with that idea? We **minimize** the risks that we feel we must take, and we avoid those that are crazy or too out of control. When we hop into the shower, for example, we take several risks. Slipping and falling probably tops the list, so we are careful not to leave the bar of soap on the floor, and perhaps we've even installed a non-skid surface in the shower. So, because we know about the risk of slipping and falling, we have stacked the deck in our favor; we have minimized the risks.

So it is in business. There are many ways to minimize the risks inherent in business. Knowledge is power. Knowing what you need to know, educating yourself by reading books like this one about the business world is a great way to minimize your risk. I will be talking about other ways to do this as well because I want you to stack the deck in your favor and to have confidence in your ability to control the amount of risk that you feel comfortable with. However, I want to be very clear that if you want to be successful in business, remember that the greatest risk of all is never taking a risk.

Will and Determination

Now, let's get to the heart and soul part of being an entrepreneur: the need to act with "considerable initiative." I'll take it deeper than that; let's call it "will and determination." It takes will and determination to make the changes in your thinking and to take the actions necessary to get to ONO. The will and determination part of the equation is something you must do for yourself, and, by the way, **will and determination can be learned.** I know this because I had to learn them; they were not traits I was born with.

I first learned will and determination through high school sports. I was always a strong athlete and could compete at the highest level. I was a four-sport letterman. However, basketball was the one sport in which my natural athleticism could not fully compensate for my lack of skill. I did not have the shooting or the ball-handling skills to make me a standout player, so I learned to earn my starting spot on the team with hard work. When I was on the floor, there was no question about who worked the hardest. I was the guy diving for every ball; I was hustling on every single play. I was doing whatever it took. When every single shot went up, I blocked out my guy. During every single fast break, I tried to be the first one down the floor. I took care of the things that I could control. That was the process that made me successful, not the skills that I brought to the table.

In summary, I want you to learn to think like an ONO entrepreneur. ONO entrepreneurs are master entrepreneurs. They are self-motivated. They act with will and determination and make the sacrifices necessary to get their own thing going, with the intent of taking control of their financial destinies. ONO entrepreneurs surround themselves with systems, products, methodologies, or investment structures that provide the means to produce income. They continually seek opportunities to find new and creative ways to make money. ONO entrepreneurs create multiple streams of income through systems that operate independently of other people and other systems.

Pride of Ownership

Have you ever noticed that we can be butting our heads against a brick wall trying to find a solution to a problem, and then, when we change just one tiny thing, we tweak the process just a little, then, wham! Everything's solved? This is just such a story.

My wife Sue and I were having trouble getting our three-year-old son, Jaken, to eat vegetables. He had the opinion that anything green didn't taste good. We knew that teaching him healthy eating was important, and were also aware of that slippery slope of forcing food on your children. We decided to try a flanking move. The solution we came up with was to create an environment where he *wanted* to eat his vegetables.

We like to garden together as a family activity. So, last year we decided to let Jaken grow his own vegetables in his own garden bed. His only understanding of the word "bed" was that it was something you sleep in. So when we told him, "This is your bed," he asked for a pillow. He kept lying down in it. We loved it.

We helped him pick out the seeds and plants for his bed. He first chose a pepper plant because he was attracted to its bright color in the picture on the packet. I warned him, "Those are spicy, Jaken." Hearing that, he quickly rejected the pepper plant, and before selecting any other vegetable, he would first ask me, "Daddy, is this one spicy?"

Jaken's chosen plants included some greens and broccoli, vegetables we previously had had a tough time getting him to eat, along with some fun, colorful plants, like purple beans. Then we planted Jaken's very own garden bed, complete with a "Jaken's Bed" sign. We had a lot of fun with it. It was a really neat family connection activity.

Jaken was proud of his little bed. He helped weed it and take care of it all spring and summer, and he often grazed while he tended. He couldn't wait until it was time to harvest. When that time came, he picked his vegetables. It was the moment-of-truth time for Sue and me; it was time to see if he would eat what he had grown.

To our relief, there was no hesitation on his part. They were *his* vegetables. He grew them, he had taken care of them, he was proud of them, and he was going to eat them. Ever since then, he has always been willing to eat his own vegetables.

It's Different When it's Yours

This same principle can be applied to a business venture. If you are an employer, a business owner, or an entrepreneur, your perspective about your business differs from an employee's. You think about a business *differently* when it's yours. That's pride of ownership.

Let's say you are a painter, an accountant, a dentist, or any occupation that requires a specific set of skills. Let's also say you work for someone else. Being an employee probably means you have opportunities to become more experienced and improve your skills. It also means you have opportunities for upward movement, higher pay, more vacation time, that sort of thing, but someone else makes the important business decisions and, of course, the profit. That's the hard part. You can become very skilled at your job and gain experience, but you are still working for someone else; you are still an employee.

Well, in the same way that Jaken had an investment in his little garden bed, if you owned that business instead of being an employee, you would have a personal investment in your own future. It's similar to the difference between a renter mentality and a homeowner mentality. A homeowner will put a little more effort into keeping the house looking good. An owner will do the paint touchup work, plant and maintain flowerbeds, and make sure the lawn is watered and mowed. He or she has that pride of ownership. I have rental houses, and the hardest thing for me to do is to find a renter who will take care of those details. It is the same in business. When it is your company or your investment venture, you do what needs to be done.

There is another factor to consider as well. If you're working for someone else, your potential is not even close to being met. I don't care how skilled you are at what you're doing or how committed you are as an employee, once you become a business owner, you'll see an animal come alive inside you that you may not even have known existed.

Once you go into the realm of entrepreneurism, you will meet this animal: your pride of ownership. So, if the fear of owning your own business is a limiting factor; if you're saying, "I don't know if I am going to be any better at this on my own," the fact is that once pride is established, you have the potential to be far better off and more productive on your own than you could possibly be working for someone else. You may want to start small at first and maybe work outside the parameters of your eight-to-five job, but the concept of ownership is something I want you to consider. As soon as you make this decision, you will experience productivity, freedom, and a power that you have never experienced before.

Make Your Fortune in Your Free Time

Being a successful entrepreneur does not necessarily mean that you have to quit your job right away and start up your own business. That is simply one way to do it. Remember, an entrepreneur is someone who uses his or her skills and creativity to produce extra income. It's a process that starts slowly and speeds up as the money builds, but I'm a firm believer that the best way to begin is while you're still working at your regular job. Creating ONO is about making your living forty hours a week and making your fortune on the weekends and in your free time.

For some of you it may be possible to mine a little extra money from your job: put in some overtime, negotiate a raise, or take on an additional project. But for most people, the prospects of that are pretty slim. Chances are that the extra income you need to produce will come from time spent outside of your job during evenings and weekends.

Tuesday Golf

Here are a couple examples of men who have made their wealth in their time off. I happen to have met both of them on the golf course on a Tuesday. I love to golf on Tuesdays. Really, any midweek day is good, but for some reason, I just prefer Tuesdays. Tuesdays are quiet days on most golf courses; there is very little course traffic. I can play at my own pace without feeling rushed by people behind me. However, my favorite thing about golfing on Tuesday is, because I go alone most of the time, I get the opportunity to meet some very interesting and helpful people. This is a tactic I use to actively participate in my own wisdom.

I learned the play-golf-and-gather-wisdom technique one Tuesday when I was paired up with a man who was, from the look of his clothes and clubs, not hurting for money. My curiosity got the better of me, so I asked him how he happened to be so blessed to be golfing on a Tuesday, a day when most of the people in the world were working. He told me he had been fortunate in investing and trading in the stock market in his spare time and now was able to quit his job and trade on the market full time. Because his schedule was flexible, he was able to golf whenever he wanted to. By the end of eighteen holes with him, I had gleaned a ton of business information.

As I was getting into my car after the round, I realized that I had just stumbled upon a gold mine. I realized that golfing on Tuesdays presented the opportunity for me to meet and make connections with people who were fortunate enough to play weekday golf, many of whom had options, not obligations. They were living the ONO lifestyle. Granted, sometimes when I ask, "How is it that you happen to be so blessed to be playing golf on a Tuesday?" I get answers like, "I work on the weekends and have the day off," but many people I meet are like the first gentleman.

Huck

One Tuesday, I bumped into a guy named Huck. I asked my question and he began to tell me about his life and how he had made his living as a school principal, but he had made his fortune in the real estate market. It turned out that he was a multi-multi-millionaire. For decades, he had made use of his summers off by buying rundown houses, fixing them up, and turning them into rentals. He had built up a "fleet" of properties over a thirty-year period. When he retired, he sold off some of his rental properties and paid for a million-dollar house in cash, but he kept some of the rentals because he really enjoys working on them. He now spends all of his free time doing the two things he loves: playing golf and fixing up houses.

Huck has ONO. He has a choice about what he does. Does he still work and maintain an income source? Sure, but *he does what he wants to do.* He could have sold all his rentals, put the money in a conservative investment vehicle and gained five percent a year. Instead, he chose to continue fixing up and renting out houses because he enjoys it.

Now *that* is ONO; that is delicious! Every one of you can and will make different choices, but my message to you is that ordinary people who come up with a meticulous plan and follow it can create fortunes in their spare time.

Think Like an Entrepreneur

- Minimize the risks you feel are worth taking, and avoid those that are too out of control.

- Will and determination are the secrets to being a successful entrepreneur.

- Pride of ownership unleashes your potential to be far more productive on your own than you could possibly be working for someone else.

- Make your living on the weekdays. Make your fortune in your free time.

Eight: Create Your ONO Account

Creating a surplus isn't only about making extra money while you're making a living. It's also about living on less than you make.

Like Huck, many people find a way to create abundance for themselves in their free time. So let's start small and create what I call an ONO account. **An ONO account is an amount of money you set aside and use to take advantage of investment opportunities when they come along.** The key to building success is creating and building that ONO account by contributing to it on a regular basis. Start now.

ONO accounts are built by creating a surplus of money and then investing it. ONO account money should only be spent on opportunities that have the potential to make you money and, at the same time, feed your wisdom. Whether your investment is in stocks, in real estate, or in continuing your education, no matter what your investment strategy is, the goal is to have your surplus money working to earn even more money.

Your ONO account will allow you to jump on an opportunity when it becomes available. For people with a lot of money in such an account, opportunity knocks almost every hour. Someone always has a great way for you to use your money that will make more money for them and for you. Having an ONO account in place and available to you at any time gives you a massive advantage, because the more you have to invest, the fewer people there will be competing with you. Put as much money as you possibly can in your ONO account each month.

Lifestyle Choices

Understand that the lifestyle choices you are making right now will have a massive impact on your future. As your income grows, don't let your spending habits rise. Keep your lifestyle at the same level and invest the growing surplus.

I believe anybody making over $20,000 a year in a secure job can mine $2,000 on the side. That's a little less than $200 a month. Everyone has the capability to spend more frugally, limit lifestyle, eliminate debt, and do whatever is needed to put $2,000 a year to work. Look at your monthly income and your spending obligations. Look for the surplus money, money that is not currently obligated. Start there.

What if you don't have much or any extra money at this point? That limitation can be overcome. Plan ahead, be creative, and make it happen. Everyone has limitations but they don't have to become stopping points that halt all forward movement. You need surplus income to start building your ONO account. There is no other way around it. With proper planning, you can create this surplus by either making more or spending less.

Most people think that they have to make more money to get to ONO and they don't see a way to do that. Remember, ONO is about changing the way you think about things. You can also get to ONO by spending less, and you can do that by making smart lifestyle choices.

Bathing in Money

A great way to explain how curbing your lifestyle can help you build your surplus account is Robert G. Allen's "Bathtub Theory." You think of your lifestyle as a bathtub. The water in the tub is the money that you have. The spout or faucet is how money comes in—that's income. The drain is where money goes out. The money going out of the drain includes the cost of the necessities of life, like food, clothing, lodging, utilities, gasoline, and insurance. The goal is to get your bathtub so full that there is a surplus of money. You want it to overflow. That surplus, the overflow, goes into your ONO account.

You get the picture. The smaller the bathtub, the easier it is to create a surplus. In order to build your ONO account, there must be a surplus of money spilling over the top of your bathtub. How do we do that and do it as quickly as possible?

The first option is to increase your income. Another option is to use the bathtub plug and decrease the amount going out a little by shopping a little more wisely. You can do that by spending less on groceries, clothes, maybe by carpooling—you know the drill. The problem is that those methods will probably make very little change in your water/money level.

How do you make a big change? Shrink your bathtub. This is the quickest way I know of to create a surplus, and it applies whether you are making $40,000 a year or $400,000 a year. **Creating a surplus isn't only about trying to make extra money while you're making a living, it's about living on less than you make.** There is a downside—the smaller the tub, the less comfortable it is. You may feel a little scrunched up as you make the necessary sacrifices. It takes some difficult choices to limit your lifestyle to create an overflow, but it will be worth it in the long run.

ONO Time

When you use your free time to earn or save money to build your ONO account, you have created what I call ONO time. This is free time you use strategically to help you get closer to reaching your goal of financial freedom. It may be taking extra time at work to acquire a new client or a new account, and then setting aside the income it brings in. It may be increasing the value of your home by putting in a little sweat equity work on the weekends. It may even be something as simple as staying home to play board games with your family on Friday night instead of going out to dinner and a movie. For a family of four, staying home rather than going out can save $100 or more.

The list of ways to spend time to earn money or save surplus money is a long one, and everyone comes up with their own variations. ONO time leads to a growing ONO account, and that leads to financial freedom. Keep that in mind at all times. When you're spending time to create wealth for yourself and your family, it becomes a great incentive and a great source of pride. It's kind of fun, too. My family loves it. When I go down to my basement office to work, I tell Jaken, "I'm going to work to make money for our family. I'm going to need about an hour of time, is that all right with you, Buddy?" Jaken will grin and say something like, "It's okay Daddy; we can wrestle later."

Delay Gratification, Build Wealth

I'd like to tell you a story with two different endings. Rae had a want. She very badly wanted a certain high-powered blender. She had seen it demonstrated over and over at different fairs and home shows, and every time she watched she wanted one even more. The blender cost almost $400, almost three times as much as the top-of-the-line models in the stores, but there seemed to be nothing it couldn't do. It could make smoothies, soup, ice cream; you name it. To make matters worse, her son and daughter each had one, and after talking with her daughter, it turned out that the blender was even more amazing then she had previously imagined. She discovered that it could even grind whole wheat for bread. Of course, Rae had not made a loaf of bread in over two years, but that was beside the point; it was a marvelous blender and she wanted one.

Rae's husband nearly went into cardiac arrest when she talked about getting one. Once the shock wore off, they discussed the possibilities and decided that it would have to wait a year. It just wasn't in the budget and, as her husband pointed out, their current blender would do just fine until then.

Imagine yourself in Rae's shoes. How would you be feeling? Sad? Angry? Jealous of those who have what you want? All of the above? You're right. She even felt a sense of loss because she had already envisioned it sitting on her kitchen counter. Do you think that after the decision to put off the purchase for a year, she wanted the super blender even more than before? You bet she did.

Now, let's look at the situation a little differently. What if the $400 blender was in the budget? Well, not exactly in the budget. Let's say Rae and her husband had an ONO account building, and they were adding $300 a month to it. It was taking some scrimping, some sacrifices, but they were doing it every month. Therefore, they could take this month's $300, and $100 from the next month's ONO account money, and they could buy that blender. So, they discussed it. What do you think they decided to do?

I hope that you are thinking like an ONO entrepreneur right now. Here is your test. Are you thinking that Rae and her husband decided *not* to buy the blender? You're right. There was no way they were going to let go of that $400. What were their feelings about *the decision not to spend the money*? You are right again. This time they were feeling proud, responsible, and in control. They were watching their ONO account grow and were exploring ways to increase it even more. Now, did Rae still want the blender? Absolutely, and she knew that she still had the option to get it in the future.

That is how wealthy people think. They put off spending money on non-necessities, so they'll have more money to spend in the future.

Wants vs. Needs

One of the great things about being an entrepreneur is the ability to control your own financial moves. You are in charge. You make the decisions. When an opportunity presents itself, you can take advantage of it if you're in a position to do so.

Americans today are so fortunate. If they make wise decisions about how they spend and save money, they can make a good living and create wealth for their families. The opportunities are there. How many people in the world do you think can even come close to doing that? Not many.

One of the biggest decisions entrepreneurs have to make very early on is what to spend money on and what *not* to spend money on. They know they have to build up an investment account, and that money has to come from somewhere, so they must come to terms with the difference between what they want and what they need. You probably already know where I'm going with this, but stick with me; I think you'll find it interesting.

The Burden of Debt

Americans don't have an earning problem. They have a spending problem. Many Americans make a good living, but they spend every penny of it. They then double their trouble with installment loans, credit card accounts and second mortgages. They put themselves in huge debt. Many spend a large percentage of their income on their *wants* rather than on their savings and investments. What makes it even worse is that too many people go into debt for their wants. In fact, most Americans would be bankrupt within 90 days if their incomes were cut off. That means they are spending a large percentage of their future income, money they haven't even earned yet. They're also increasing their debt and paying interest on it. That's a scary thought. Scarier still is the fact that many people have a tough time telling the difference between their wants and the necessities of life, their *needs*.

We have all heard the solution to this is to construct a budget, and for those of you who have successfully done this, my hat is off to you. I've never been able to do it. I've never been able to construct it, let alone follow through with it. My problem always showed up at the point of purchase. I needed help deciding whether or not to buy something. My budget never helped me with this; in fact, I found myself rebelling against it because I felt badly about saying no to the things I wanted.

The confusion over spending money on the things we want rather than the things we need is complicated even further by our *NEED* (I'm using the term deliberately) for immediate gratification. We want it, and we want it *now*. The problem is that most of us were never taught the difference between wants and needs and we feel some negative emotions when we have to give up or even delay buying something we want.

To complicate matters even further, a huge number of Americans are addicted to spending money, but don't realize it. I have fought all sorts of addictions in my life, and I have learned to recognize and to arrest them. So, my way of controlling my addiction to spending, as well as combating my immediate gratification instincts, AND my determination to spend money on needs rather than wants, is what I call my "Nah" response. It's really the precursor to the larger scale version of my saving and investing lifestyle strategy. It sounds simple, but it has changed my life.

Think Before You Spend

When I am tempted to buy something, it rings a bell in my head. Believe me, there are hundreds of those *somethings* in my life. Sporting goods stores are a nightmare for me, but I have trained myself to evaluate the consequences of my actions and to run them through my decision filters. If there are any negative implications in the purchase I'm considering, I simply say, "Nah, I'm fine without it." Then I turn and walk away *without remorse*. This technique is about more than the words I say, it is about being at peace and moving toward ONO.

Those are the kinds of decisions that thrifty, forward-looking people make. If you can give up the little things now, up front, you can enjoy much bigger things later on, like the really BIG one, fulfilling your Higher Purpose. If you can't deal with delaying your wants financially, you will be like so many Americans, probably in the hole, working thirty to forty years with very little to show for it. These people have sacrificed their long-term wants, their dreams, for immediate ones. These are the retired people who have always wanted to travel, but who cannot afford the gas, let alone the RV.

Mining for Money

To move down the path toward creating their fortunes, wealthy people begin by creating a surplus within the framework of their existing lifestyles.

When we consider all the things we spend money on each month, and, of course, when we dream about all the things we want to spend money on, it's tough to figure out the difference between what we need and what we want. I really believe that your family's future financial success hinges on your knowing the difference between the two. **You need to be very clear about where you *need* to spend your money and where you *want* to spend your money.**

Trimming Expenses

Needs include things like groceries, clothing, and car payments, and **wants** would be things like a new sofa, eating out twice a week, or going on a family vacation. Everything, every dollar you have spent, are currently spending, or anticipate spending is either a want or a need: your utility bill, birthday presents for the kids, the washing machine you financed over the last twelve months, going out for a dinner and a movie, or the hospital bill for the new baby.

Now here's an eye-opener. Think about the money you spend on needs each month and ask yourself whether there are places where you could spend a little less money. How large is your house? A family of four could certainly make a 1500-square-foot house work for them, but lots of people are burning their surplus money by insisting on 3000 square feet or more.

You can also find huge savings by looking at family vacations, Christmas spending, the car you drive, where and how often you buy your clothes, and how often you eat out. You can save a lot of money by eating out less, not to mention the benefits to your family from gathering around the table for some home-cooked food and great conversation.

Remember my premise is that Americans don't have an earning problem, they have a spending problem. You need to spend money on a car, that is a given, but there may be a huge difference between the car you need and the car you want. Don't worry, I'm not going to tell you that the way to get wealthy is to go down to the junkyard and pick up Jed Clampet's rig with the optional rocker for Granny on top.

The BMW or the Honda?

Let's be reasonable. Let's assume you are in a position where it is necessary for you to look good and you need to drive an attractive car. Let's also say that, like every other businessperson in the world, you really want to drive a brand new luxury vehicle, and your choice is an entry level BMW sedan that would cost you $35,000. You have $11,000 cash for a down payment, and you can afford payments on the remaining $24,000 if you really stretch yourself thin. Unfortunately, driving a new BMW is not going to help you build wealth.

So, you've determined the car you *want*; now let's get down to the car you *really need*. You need a car that looks nice and is dependable. A five or six-year-old used Honda Accord will suit all those needs and you can pay for it in cash with your $11,000. Granted, there's a huge difference between a BMW and a Honda, and the car you really need may fall somewhere in between the two, but for the purpose of this example, let's use the Honda.

Also, before we get into this, I want to acknowledge the fact that some businesses and occupations do require a nice car. This is a different situation because the quality of your car is a necessity, which makes it an investment and throws it into the "needs" category. When all is said and done, it's still about deciding between needs and wants, so let's move on.

You'll be sacrificing the BMW for a car that is still nice, costs much less, and won't need to be financed. With this move, you'll be cutting back on the spending, but you will not actually be putting any money in your account, so let's take this scenario one step further. Take the $24,000 you would have had to finance for the BMW (my frugal grandmother would roll over in her grave) and, although we've already seen that this would be a stretch for you, take the monthly payment that you would have had to make on a monthly basis for six years and *put that $444 payment in your ONO account every month*. I've run the numbers for you in the next section, but after six years of saving and investing that $444, you will have well over $40,000. Now, this is about as subtle as a bad toupee, but can you see how the sacrifice you were willing to make to own a car that you *wanted* could become a sacrifice that you make to take you and your family closer to ONO?

Spending Less and Saving More

Just because seventy percent of the American economy is based on consumer spending doesn't mean that your family has to be responsible for a large part of that.

Be frugal. Decide what you truly need and spend money for those things. Curb spending money on wants and put it into your ONO Account.

Involve all the players. This is a critical piece of the Family First Entrepreneurial picture. Have your spouse *and* your kids help make decisions about saving and spending money. If you do not have your family on board at this point in the process, they'll never be with you to make other important financial decisions like going camping instead of going to Disneyland for a week.

Have fun! I have three life goals and I'll discuss them in greater length later on, but I want to mention them briefly now. They are to love, to learn, and to live life with joy. Adopt them for yourself during this important decision making shift. Laugh. Celebrate the learning. It's okay to chuckle about that DeWalt 18 volt cordless drill that fills you with lust every time you go to Home Depot. Have fun making spending and saving decisions because they are all about loving your family. You're doing it because you want a delicious life for them.

Most importantly, be at peace with your decisions. If you can make peace with delaying or sacrificing your wants, you will find it so much easier to make wise business decisions. You won't suffer those feelings of loss or resentment. The way to change the way you feel about giving up some of your wants now is to *change the way you think about it.*

Until I changed the way I thought about spending money, I would walk into the store, and I wanted *everything*. I had no money, but I wanted to buy everything I liked and often bought things I couldn't afford. Later, when I was delaying my wants to build my ONO account, I would go into a store, look at the things I wanted, and I could gladly pass up the opportunity to buy them. In fact, I'd do it with a smile on my face. I could do that because I had an ONO account that was building. **I was actually making money from the money I had saved by delaying the purchase of my wants.** That was very exciting for me.

If you and your family can separate your wants from you needs and delay or give up spending money on your wants, you will:

- Build long-term wealth and opportunities for yourself and your family.

- Have started your children down their own path to ONO.

- Have more of your wants fulfilled over the course your lifetime because you will have more money.

- Have more free time because you will not have had to work as long during your lifetime.

~ *Opportunity for Reflection* ~

Make a list of the items you possess that you now wish you had not bought. After each, write the negative impact it has had on your life.

_____   _____

_____   _____

_____   _____

_____   _____

_____   _____

_____   _____

_____   _____

Create Your ONO Account

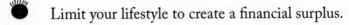

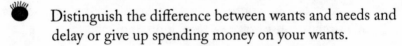

Limit your lifestyle to create a financial surplus.

Distinguish the difference between wants and needs and delay or give up spending money on your wants.

No matter what the rest of the world is doing, remember that the keys to wealth are saving and investing, not spending.

Nine: Proof in Numbers

It's not about how much money you make,
it's about how much you save and invest.

The Power of Compounding Interest

A person can build a great ONO account by simple, yet habitual, saving and investing. Let's look at a man who begins building his ONO account at the age of twenty:

- Through the cutting back of wants, he finds a way to save $200 a month and does so religiously for ten years.

- On top of saving, he finds entrepreneurial ways to invest and earns a ten percent yearly return on his money.

- By the age of thirty, he is making better money and decides to double the amount he saves each month.

- He again doubles that amount at the age of forty to $800 a month.

Now, though it may not sound like a ton of money, let's do a little math with those numbers to see what kind of situation our friend is in by the age of fifty.

Description	Time Period (in Years)	Income Saved Yearly (Invested Monthly)	Return on Investment	Total Return	ONO Account Balance
Age 20-29 Invests $200/month	10	$2,400	10%	$40,969	**$40,969**
Age 30-39 Invests $400/month	10	$4,800	10%	$81,937	**$192,842**
Age 40-49 Invests $800/month	10	$9,600	10%	$163,875	**$685,909**

By the time our friend is fifty years old, he will have invested $168,000 of his earned income over this thirty-year time span. Through shrewd investments, he has turned his $168,000 into nearly $686,000, and, of course, the investment and return possibilities on that amount of money are endless. He has the choice to invest some of it in high-risk ventures with the potential of high rewards and keep the other portion in low risk investments. Once you have money, making money from your money is easy. With discipline and planning, saving money really isn't that hard to do either.

Wally and Fred

Let's pursue this idea a little further. In a second scenario, we have two fellows, Wanting Wally and Frugal Fred. They'll show you how delaying wants now will pay off *big time* later.

Wanting Wally works 60 hours a week as a salesman, makes $80,000 a year, and has every toy he ever wanted. Because of his spending habits, he has limited himself to investing $2,500 a year, and that is only because his accountant reminds him to fund his IRA. Because he has no spare time, Wally isn't able to work his investments entrepreneurially which then affects his return on those investments, so he earns an average of 5%. He can afford some of his wants, but because he has so many, he has to borrow at an interest rate of 10 percent to purchase the rest. Because of this, he has an annual net loss year after year, but he has a lot of nice stuff to show for it.

Now take Frugal Fred. He works 40 hours a week in a welding shop as a machinist making $36,000 a year. Fred is very conscientious and tries to save as much as possible. Through his efforts, he saves $6,000 a year and lives on the rest. He buys used cars, dresses conservatively, and lives a happy, yet thrifty, lifestyle. Over time, that $6,000 a year will increase at an incredible rate because Fred made it his business to learn how to invest it and to be wise with his money.

Description	Time Period (in Years)	Income Saved Yearly (Invested Monthly)	Return on Investment	Total
Wanting Wally Salary of $80,000/year	30	**$2,500**	5%	**$310,491**
Frugal Fred Salary of $36,000/year	30	**$6,000**	10%	**$1,130,243**

Wally may have the higher paying job, the material possessions to show for it, and after 30 years, he may have over $300,000 in his IRA, but unfortunately, the amount of money he has borrowed and paid in interest to fulfill his wants far outweighs his retirement account.

Fred on the other hand—even without the high-profile, high-paying job—has created wealth for himself. His financial wisdom and discipline allowed him to end up with over a million dollars in the bank. In other words, Fred has options to do whatever he wants, whenever he wants to do it. All it took was a little patience and careful planning.

Two Extremes

Now some of you may be thinking that old Fred led a boring life for 30 years while he was accumulating his wealth. He never had any fun and he didn't have any nice things. You may be correct, but remember that I used him as an example at one end of a scale. I showed you what was *possible* if you made huge sacrifices to build wealth. I also gave you an example of the other extreme—Wanting Wally. Unfortunately, the Wally example is not as far-fetched as you'd think. There are millions of people like Wanting Wally alive today.

Let's get back to Fred. Let's paint a picture with a little more balance. We'll put Fred in a scenario where his wife spends ten hours a week working entrepreneurially from home. She earns the family's fun money. At fifteen dollars per hour, she can put 600 dollars worth of fun into the equation and now Fred's family has a little more balance.

I'm not asking you to deprive yourself of the good things. I'm asking you to consider how much they really cost and then, instead of "deprive," use the word, "limit." Limit spending, save money and invest it entrepreneurially to build wealth.

Save by Limiting Lifestyle

By now, it's clear that investing money over time reaps huge rewards. Now, let's get down to the details of how to start accumulating that money. Let's talk about simple things like buying a cup of coffee or eating out.

Description	Time Period (in Years)	Income Saved Yearly (Invested Monthly)	Return on Investment	Total
Buying coffee every workday at a convenience store for $.50 vs. paying $4.00 at a gourmet coffee shop	30	$3.50 a day for 250 days = $875	10%	$164,837
Staying home and cooking a meal for two ($10.00 + time & energy) vs. going out to eat ($35.00) 3 times a week	30	$25 saved 3x/week for one year = $3,900	10%	$734,658

The numbers are staggering aren't they? Now, remember the BMW vs. Honda situation we talked about earlier? Let's look at that again. Let's see what would happen if, instead of financing $24,000 to get the BMW, you bought the Honda with cash and invested what you would have spent in finance payments.

Car	Cost	Amount Financed	Finance Rate	Finance Period (in months)	Total Paid (monthly)
BMW	$35,000	$24,000	10%	72	$444.62
Honda	$11,000	$0	0%	0	$0

Car	Cost	Invested Savings (monthly)	Time Period (months)	Return on Investment	Total available in ONO account
BMW	$35,000	$0	72	0%	$0
Honda	$11,000	$444.62	72	10%	$43,662.25

In either of these scenarios, you use a total of $43,012 of your income over a six-year period:

1. You can spend the $43,012 on your car and own a BMW that six years later, after depreciation, is worth about $17,000. This pencils out to a net loss of just over $26,000.

On the other hand,

2. You can spend $11,000 and own a Honda Accord which in six years, after depreciation, will be worth about $6,000. You could invest the $444.62 that you would be spending every month in finance payments. In the end, in addition to having a car worth $6,000, you also have an additional $43,662.25 in an investment account.

Now, when you compare the two situations, the person who bought the Honda ends up with $32,000 more than the person who bought the BMW. To take it one step further, invest that $32,000 for thirty years and calculate what the BMW owner is sacrificing. Don't want to do the math? Let me do it for you. $32,000 invested at 10 percent for 30 years equals $634,796. Look at the impact that just one smart spending choice can have on your life.

Still want the BMW? I didn't think so.

Earn Time by Delaying Wants

Before you start getting all excited about saving, let me tell you that it gets even better. I've told you that delaying your wants will create more money, but better yet, it will also create more free time because you won't have to work as long. Let me prove that to you.

Mr. Spender and Mr. ONO are two men who were originally in the same situation, but because of their different thinking styles about financial management, they have found themselves living very different lifestyles. Mr. Spender indulges all his wants, all of the time. Mr. ONO, on the other hand, delays fulfilling his wants and instead invests that saved money for the future. This table shows the difference that a little saving can make over a thirty-year span, both in terms of your finances and in terms of your free time.

Description	First 10 years on the job Salary $45,000/year	Second 10 years on the job Salary $55,000/year	Third 10 years on the job Salary $65,000/year
Mr. Spender	Works 9-5 Monday-Friday	Works 9-5 Monday-Friday	Works 9-5 Monday-Friday
	Fulfills all of his wants and invests $0	Fulfills all of his wants and invests $0	Fulfills all of his wants and invests $0
Mr. ONO	Works 9-5 Monday-Friday	Works 9-5 Monday-Thursday	Stays home
	Fulfills none of his wants and invests $400/month	Fulfills some of his wants and invests $500/month	Fulfills all of his wants

Description	First 10 Years	Second 10 Years	Third 10 Years	Return on Investment	ONO Account Balance
Mr. Spender 30 yrs. on the job 60,000 hrs. worked	$0 Invested	$0 Invested	$0 Invested	10%	$0
Mr. ONO 20 yrs. on the job 36,000 hrs. worked	$54,000 Invested	$66,000 Invested	$0 Invested	10%	$877,709

After 30 years, Mr. ONO has accumulated over $877,000 in his ONO account, without saving a dime during the last ten years. Mr. Spender has $0. While Mr. Spender looks more successful in terms of his material possessions, he now has to continue working for 10 years longer than Mr. ONO just to meet his needs and pay his debts.

Mr. ONO, on the other hand, has the opportunity to continue investing. He's retired and he can spend time doing what he wants, when he wants. Over 30 years, Mr. ONO works 24,000 fewer hours than Mr. Spender. Mr. ONO has created free time for himself by putting off buying wants until he could afford them.

On the Lookout

One of the greatest adventures and most enjoyable aspects of an entrepreneurial career for me has been the search for new venture opportunities. I love hunting for new ways to make money. There's a lot that goes into the process of evaluating a potential venture possibility. Finding the type of endeavor that works for me, doing the groundwork, the due diligence, evaluating the potential profits, looking at the risks, and making it work by being creative are all things that can really be enjoyable if you know how to approach them. It starts with the excitement that comes from being on the lookout.

As you build your ONO account, you will automatically begin to think about ways to make your money start working for you. There are so many possibilities. The feeling when I am searching for a new venture is hard to describe, but it's thrilling. It's about adrenaline and anticipation, it's about opportunities and putting a puzzle together, it's about developing a new source of income, and it's about pride. I am proud of the fact that I'm looking for new ways to earn financial security for my family. More than anything, it's about the thrill of the hunt. Believe me, you'll love it.

Proof in Numbers

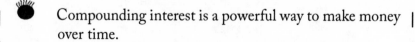 Compounding interest is a powerful way to make money over time.

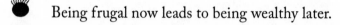 Being frugal now leads to being wealthy later.

Do the math—consider how every dollar you spend or save affects your long-term goals.

Be on the lookout for new entrepreneurial ventures.

Ten: Creative Entrepreneurism

Limitations can be overcome with creativity.

In a recent conversation with my friends, Aaron and Sara, I was sharing my thoughts about how to acquire wealth by limiting your lifestyle and delaying your wants. Aaron is an entrepreneur in pursuit of wealth and was on board with all of my theories. But when I started talking about making hard decisions when choosing a car, both he and Sara started grinning. Sara then said, "That sacrifice can be overcome by creativity; I know from personal experience." I was intrigued and asked her to tell her story.

Sara took me back several years to the time when Aaron had just quit his corporate job to pursue an entrepreneurial business venture. They knew there were better things in store for him in an independently owned business. However, there were sacrifices that had to be made with the career change, and the largest of these was giving back his company-issued vehicle. Because of this, he, Sara and their three young children had only one car and they were not in a financial position to buy another one, even a used one.

Sara was supportive and willing to make the sacrifices necessary, but this particular one was especially hard on her. Aaron needed the car to do service calls all day and Sara was left at home with the kids and without a vehicle. For eight months, they lived like that. Sara had to wait until Aaron came home at night to use the car.

During the day, she had to rely on friends to give her rides to the grocery store and to take their kids to soccer practice.

Inspiration Strikes

One day while Sara was online, a pop-up appeared at the top of the screen that read, "Get a Free Car!" On any normal day, she would have rolled her eyes at the obvious gimmick, closed the pop-up, and continued with her business. But, because of her I-need-a-car-so-badly-I-can-hardly-stand-it status, her curiosity got the best of her and she clicked on the pop-up. As she browsed the website, she found out there were companies willing to give you a car if you would let them "wrap" it, that is, put a giant vinyl sticker around the entire car with the company's logo on it for advertising purposes.

This particular website wanted people to pay them to find a company willing to do this, and there was a six-to-twelve-month waiting period. Because of that, this particular program wouldn't work for Sara, but it did spark an idea.

Sara ran with the idea of trying to get a company to buy and wrap a car for her. She put in hours of research on the Internet and began to call local business establishments. Her first few calls led to dead ends, but finally, a local car dealership agreed to discuss her idea. She approached the sales manager with her story, her plan, and her research. After several days of discussion and bargaining, the dealership agreed to set Sara up with a car wrapped with their advertisements. In fact, they even threw in leather seats and a DVD player upgrade. In turn, Aaron and Sara agreed to buy the car on the company's five-year finance plan and, for the first two years, the dealership made the payments in exchange for the advertising wrap.

Thanks to her ingenuity and determination, Sara took matters into her own hands and overcame their problems without putting the family's financial situation in jeopardy.

Another one of my favorite things about this story is the way Sara was supportive of Aaron's desire to pursue an entrepreneurial career. They both knew the sacrifices their family needed to make, and they were both committed to the decision. It is so important for husbands and wives to be on the same page when it comes to business and finances. Statistics in the book, *The Millionaire Next Door* by Thomas Stanley and William Danko, indicate that if one spouse is a saver and the other is a spender, the couple has a much lower chance of financial success than when both share the value of saving. For an entrepreneurial career to work, both spouses need to commit to making it work.

Enjoy the Process

At this point, I certainly hope you're not thinking that the only time you can really enjoy life is once you have reached ONO, or that the process of creating opportunity is nothing but sacrifice and hard work. My own process of becoming an entrepreneur and creating success for my family and myself was exciting and a lot of fun. That's largely because we made a conscious decision to make it that way. Sure, there were tough times. I can remember several times in the last fifteen years when I have said to myself, "Man, life is living me right now, I'm not living life." There will be times like that for you as well. Remember, this process is about you taking control of the footwork, and one of the few things that you will always be able to control is your attitude.

When I first made the decision to get a grip on my life and really pursue wealth, I made a promise to myself that I would become financially successful, but I would not allow the pursuit of money take over our lives. This was during a time of huge spiritual growth for me. After a lot of thought, prayer, and reading, I came to the realization that, at the end of my life, there were only two questions that mattered. They were, "Whom did you love?" and "What did you learn?" I wrote a motto for my life based on those two important goals, "To love and to learn." I found that by keeping those two things *on the top shelf of my life*, I could pursue other goals and everything would work out just fine.

Live Life With Joy

One day I was discussing life and business with a gentleman who asked me what my aspirations were. I answered, "I want to be in a place where I am free from financial burdens, but most importantly, my goals are to love and to learn." He looked at me with a grin and said, "Aren't you forgetting something? You must also enjoy the process. You have to live life with joy."

That's when it hit me. I realized that we are limited in the time we have here on earth, and we must take advantage of every moment. My new motto became, "To love, to learn, and to live life with joy."

To keep myself true to my motto, I have made it a point to surround myself with people who live by the same standards. One of those people, Orville Thompson, has become a great friend, a mentor, and a business associate. He is a great model of how to manage the balance between your personal life and your business life. He is kind, spiritual, fair, and honest in all his business dealings. Anyone who has ever done business with him will tell you the same thing.

I once asked Orville what he wanted out of life. He answered, "I just want enough money to be comfortable. I want a nice home for my family. I want to be able to put my kids through good schools, and I want to have time to spend with them." To round it off, Orville finished with, "I also always want to be able to drink high-grade root-beer."

Though he may not have used my words, he had the same idea; he is devoted to loving, learning, and living life with joy; he enjoys the process. Orville has taught me to stay light-hearted; I try to keep a good attitude. It goes back to the things that I can control and the things that I cannot. I can control my attitude. So I do. It's that simple.

Stay Upbeat

Another part of enjoying the process of being an entrepreneur is learning not to get down on yourself or give up when times get tough. I learned this lesson one day, but not in a business setting. It came to me on the golf course.

Five years ago, I decided to learn to play golf. Now, I have always been a natural athlete; I've been involved in sports my entire life: volleyball, tennis, even football and baseball in college. Every other sport I had tried came easily to me, so I assumed golf would be the same. Big mistake. I have now been playing golf for five years and am just starting to stabilize my game; it's been a tough challenge.

When I first started playing, I was constantly frustrated because no matter what I did, I could not hit the ball straight. After a few rounds, I knew that I couldn't figure the game out on my own, so I went to my friend and avid golfer, Clive Johnston, for advice. Clive taught me the basics: the grip, the stance, the swing. But most importantly, he taught me the mental approach to the game. He saw my aggravation when things weren't going right, and said to me, "Marc, if you want to learn to love the game of golf, you've got to learn to enjoy the process of recovery. If you hit a bad shot, rather than getting all frustrated, what you need to do is get excited about the challenge of getting out of that place and back on to the short grass."

Like golf, business has plenty of ups and downs. The key to success is keeping a positive attitude in the low times. So many people give up the moment things stop going their way. In order to be successful, you have to acknowledge that things could be better and that you are having a challenge or two. Then, instead of throwing in the towel, get excited about how you are going to recover and get to that better place. Believe that every challenge presents an opportunity to learn to be creative and the potential to produce new wealth.

> Orville and Clive taught me the secrets to finding joy and keeping it in my life:
>
> - Don't let yourself be burdened by things around you or by a negative attitude.
>
> - Know that you are in control of your own attitude at all times.
>
> - Shoulder that responsibility and take pride in your efforts.
>
> - Be open to every challenge and know that you can overcome it.
>
> - Most important, be optimistic about everything that you do. Enjoy the process of building wealth and striving to reach that place of ONO. Live life with joy.

Jaken's Everest Moment

I took my oldest son Jaken hiking one day. On our way up the trail, Jaken spotted what he called a "humongous" rock. It was actually about eight feet tall, but when you're only three feet tall, eight feet seems way up there. As soon as Jaken saw the rock, he wanted to climb it, and he was determined to do it all by himself.

As he began his ascent, I stood right next to him and coached him through the climb. I told him where to grab on with his hands and where the best footholds were. Finally, he had climbed just high enough so his hands could reach the top, but he was having trouble finding a foothold that would give him that final boost. Being the helpful father I am, I reached up and placed his foot on a secure outcropping. Wrong move, Dad.

When Jaken felt my hand on his foot, he lost it. He had started out thrilled by the idea of accomplishing this feat on his own. The fact that I helped him, even if it was just a tiny nudge, broke his heart. He lost all desire to get to the top and started to cry. I helped him down and tried my best to calm him. I realized that Jaken had not perceived my assistance as help. It had crumpled his will and determination and ruined his plan for a solo triumph.

By Myself!

What happened next changed everything. As soon as he calmed down, Jaken headed right back up that rock. He was not about to quit. I had learned my lesson the first time, so there was no way I was going to help him this time unless he asked for it. He reached the spot where I had helped him the last time, and he paused. Then with a little grunt, he used all of his strength to get his foot onto that rock, and pulled himself to the top. With a giant smile on his face, he raised his arms above his head in triumph, and he exclaimed, "I did it! I did it all by myself!"

After Jaken let out his call of triumph, I assumed he would step back onto the large, flat part of the rock where he could stand safely. To my dismay, he did the opposite and inched closer to the edge, so close that his toes were hanging over the edge of the sheer eight-foot wall. He didn't seem to care. He just stood there, smiling. I stood below, getting more and more nervous. I told him to step back, but he stayed on the edge and continued to gaze off into the distance. I cautioned him again and told him to step back. This time he responded, "Wait a second Daddy, I'm looking at the view."

Jaken taught me two very important lessons that day. The first one is obvious. Ask for help if you need it, but savor the power and growth in doing the tough stuff by yourself. The second is one that so many of us forget to do. Jaken took the time to look around, take in his surroundings, and be proud of his accomplishments. Not only that, he rewarded himself for a job well done.

Smell the Roses

As you work your way toward ONO, make sure to reward yourself as well. Your ultimate goal is ONO, but you also need to set short-term goals and reward yourself when you reach them. On our hike, the ultimate goal was to reach the end of the trail at the top of the hill, but Jaken made a smaller goal for himself, and when he accomplished it, he rewarded himself.

As humans, we need affirmation and encouragement to keep us motivated. Some of that affirmation has to come from within. Keep telling yourself that you can make it, and when you do make it, celebrate.

Set goals for yourself and when you meet them, give yourself a pat on the back and have some fun. Your rewards do not have to be material possessions. In fact, some of the best rewards are experiential. Take your family on a picnic or visit a park. Indulge in a long, hot bath or take the time to watch a sunset.

Give yourself a moment to *feel rewarded* and bask in that sense of accomplishment. Never forget where you started. Take the time to look back and reflect. Don't wait until you get to the top of the hill to look at the view. Find rocks along the way, climb them, take satisfaction in what you have done, and enjoy the view. Get reenergized, and most important, keep marching up that hill to your ultimate goal—to ONO.

~ *Opportunity for Reflection* ~

List meaningful ways to reward yourself without spending much money.

_____

_____

_____

_____

_____

_____

_____

Creative Entrepreneurism

- Independent ownership creates pride and allows you to maximize your potential.

- Be entrepreneurially creative.

- Find meaningful ways to reward yourself and your family without spending a lot of money.

- Building wealth through entrepreneurism is fun. Love, learn, and live life with joy.

Eleven: Imitation, Not Innovation

"Successful people ask better questions, and as a result, they get better answers."

~Anthony Robbins

As you start to plan your path to ONO, take a moment to look around and observe people who are already there. Notice the couple who spent eighteen months in Brazil doing service work for their church. Then there's the man who still spends a few hours at his place of work, but uses some of his free time learning two foreign languages, taking tango lessons with his wife, and volunteering in the food service line at the local homeless shelter. And don't forget the couple who retired early, really early, and who now spend their time doing whatever they like.

How did all these people get to ONO? I'll bet if you ask them, you'll find out the same thing I found out. They didn't reinvent the wheel. Instead, they followed the example of what someone else had already done.

"Catchin' Anything?"

If we look closely at ourselves, and if we reach back through stories and see ourselves as our parents and grandparents saw us when we were four or five years old, we would realize that we haven't changed much. I was always a curious kid growing up and was never shy. I asked a lot of people a lot of questions. At age four, I used to drive my parents crazy at restaurants because before I ordered, I'd walk around the restaurant and ask people, "Whatcha' eatin'?" and then, "Is it good?"

My mom, ever the manners monitor, hated this. But no matter how many times she told me not to be so nosy, I persisted, especially on family fishing trips. Before my parents would even get out of the truck, I'd be down chatting with all the guys fishing from the bank. First question (very appropriate, I think) was always, "Catchin' anything?" Second question: "Whatcha' usin' for bait?"

It worked every time. My instinctive behavior saved me the trouble of having to wade through all of my options. I would find out what worked and then jump on the bandwagon.

As you make your way down the path toward ONO, you'll be amazed at how much wasted time and energy you can save yourself by learning from others who have gone before you. So, if people are *successful* at something you want to do, ask them what they are doing. Similarly, if people are *not successful* at something you want to do, ask them the same question. You will save yourself a lot of time and effort.

Guessing at Normalcy

Almost fifteen years ago, I stumbled across a concept that explained a lot for me. I'm talking about the Adult Child of an Alcoholic Syndrome (ACOA).

I have alcoholic grandparents on both sides of my family tree. I was also an alcoholic. I got sober in 1992. Neither of my parents were alcoholics, but both of them were raised in troubled alcoholic homes. Because their own upbringing was the only exposure to parenting they ever had, they raised my sister and me the way they were raised. That's generally what happens. It's instinct. I don't blame my parents. I believe they were doing their best, but what happened, happened. Learning about being an ACOA helped me to understand myself better and made me determined to try to break that cycle with my own children.

What happened because of my upbringing, as well as my own alcoholism, was that when I left home I had no idea of what normal looked like. What is normal? What should I be doing? I didn't have a clear definition; I had to guess at what appropriate behaviors might be. To double my trouble, I made some very poor guesses. I never quite knew what direction I should take.

I find that in society, many people are searching for normalcy. My personal battles were as unique to me as yours are to you. You need to adopt an "identify and conquer" mentality when considering your own personal growth. This is the story of how I overcame things in my life from which many people never recover. If I can do it, so can you.

In Cheyenne

Two huge things happened to me almost simultaneously. I moved away from my home in Boise, Idaho and I took on a new and terribly hard job in Cheyenne, Wyoming. I was fresh and raw at that time in my life. I was in a new area. I had no friends, and I was trying to break out of my old habits and get a grip on who I really was. I was so scattered. I didn't know anything anymore. Everything I thought I had known before no longer seemed to work.

I looked around for a better way and found Alcoholics Anonymous. I will tell you today with no shame whatsoever that the man I am today is the product of two "houses," one was the House of Amway, which I will get to in the next section, and the other was the House of Alcoholics Anonymous. In AA, I learned to build relationships, real relationships. As an alcoholic, I had been selfish and self-serving. I learned through AA to be of value to others, to seek out good people to be my friends, and to be generous. Best of all, I learned to listen—to really hear what people were saying. I had always been an observant person and AA helped me to build on that with a new ability to listen.

Once I got sober, I started to straighten up my life. I discovered three skills that helped me in my quest for normalcy. The first was learning to read for information. The second was to go back to my instinctive behavior as a child. I talked to people who had more wisdom than I did, and (this is where my AA training kicked in) I *listened* to their answers. I found that the more closely I listened, the more I could actually "read" them. I noticed their body language and their facial expressions, and I could "sense" much more information than their mere words were providing. The third skill followed naturally: I watched people and noticed what worked for them.

For seven years, I took my search for information very seriously. I got rid of my TV and I literally read hundreds of books and talked to hundreds of people with the intent and purpose of gaining from their wisdom.

That is when I coined the phrase, "Be an active participant in your own wisdom." The operative term here is "active." I think we must aggressively pursue the information we need to move forward with any project.

My project, the quest for normalcy, became a quest for so much more—it became a quest for success. **I found out from that quest that I wanted to be a moral and ethical man, a good businessman, and a great friend—I wanted to be a *success* in all parts of my life in the finest definition of the word.** I learned to look for men and women who were successful in those areas, and began to imitate what they were doing to achieve their success.

As I write this book, I freely admit that even though I have learned these skills and adapted them to my life and business practices, I am far from perfect at using them. I am still in the process. Like every growth-minded person in the world, I strive for excellence but never arrive at perfection, and I feel blessed to know the difference.

~ *Opportunity for Reflection* ~

List how you could improve your life by cutting your TV time in half.

_____   _____

_____   _____

_____   _____

_____   _____

Become a Reader

I mentioned earlier that two houses helped shape the man I have become. The second part of this story is about the House of Amway. This was one of those, "When it seemed like things couldn't get any worse, a gift came out of the blue," experiences, and it completely changed my life.

I was twenty-two and sober. I had taken a job working for the National Federation of Independent Business (NFIB) and, as I told you before, I was in Cheyenne, away from my home and friends for the first time. My job involved going from business to business, soliciting renewals and new sales. I'll tell you what, it was tough. It took every ounce of courage I had, day in and day out, just to walk into the next business.

One day, I called on an NFIB member who told me that he wanted to talk to me about a business opportunity. It turned out to be an Amway presentation. I had never been approached by a network marketing organization before, so I had no preconceptions. I listened with an open mind and found the program very appealing. It wasn't necessarily the presentation or the program that appealed to me; it was the man. I was intrigued by his integrity and sincerity. His name was Troy Hine. Troy was a family-oriented man who owned an auto body shop and had built a very successful Amway business on the side.

A Mentor

I found a friend and mentor in Troy. I was able to share my stories, good and bad, and I was free to vent my frustrations with him. He listened to me, encouraged me, and gave me the moral support that was so critical to me at that time. Because of Troy's kindness and willingness to listen to what I had to say, I became interested in what he had to say and agreed to become part of Amway.

As a new Amway member, I was strongly encouraged to order two educational and motivational audio tapes, along with several books from an endorsed reading list every two weeks. The tapes and books covered all sorts of topics—how to be an ethical man in life and business, how to be service oriented, how to look beyond yourself, how to practice delayed gratification, how to be a learner, and on, and on, and on.

I embraced it all. The timing was perfect for me. I threw away my TV and became one hundred percent committed to learning.

I was a lonely guy there in Cheyenne, Wyoming. I was no longer drinking. I didn't know anybody, so I just crawled into my learning cave and fed my mind. I fed my mind while I was driving on the road with those incredible books on tape, and when I was in my apartment at night or on the weekends, I fed my mind with books.

Because I was so wrapped up in getting my life in order, I never really became active in Troy's organization and left after about a year. However, in Amway I learned about the power of a network marketing system. I also learned about residual income, multiple streams of income, and the relationship between time and money. I still consider network marketing to be one of the best opportunities for undercapitalized entrepreneurs to build sideline income streams, which is a key part of the ONO strategy.

From that time onward, it became very clear to me that I needed to be an active participant in my own wisdom. Traditionally, we think of gaining wisdom through experience; but if we tweak that a little, we realize that we all can take deliberate steps to gain wisdom. We can make it a daily, methodical activity: setting appointments, making phone calls, and building relationships with people wiser than ourselves. Ask questions, listen closely to the answers, and, more important, listen to what lies beneath the answers. You can get to ONO more quickly if you learn from the people who have gone down the road before you.

Even though I never sponsored one person during my time with Amway, I ate their information up. I read every book they suggested, and I listened to every tape they could give me. They said, "Leaders are readers," and I took that literally and made it true for myself. It was so influential in guiding me to be the man that I am today that I couldn't possibly calculate the return on my investment. It's enormous, both financially and personally.

I still read a lot. I am always on the lookout for interesting authors. What I find is that there is generally one key concept, one gem in every book. I would challenge you to read a minimum of one informational book every month.

Signs

On the path to ONO, there are signs along the way to guide you. One sign says, **"Look for the gems."** Another big sign bordered with flashing lights is posted at the beginning of the path and at several other points along the way. It says, **"Be a reader! Learn from the knowledge and experience of others."**

Imitation not Innovation

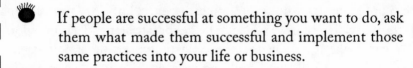 If people are successful at something you want to do, ask them what made them successful and implement those same practices into your life or business.

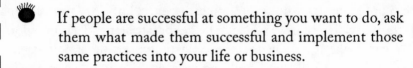 Watch and listen for gems. Take those ideas and build systems around them that will work in your life.

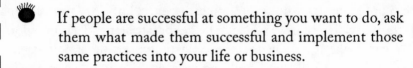 Constantly feed your mind. Books are a great source of mental nutrition and inspiration. For my list of suggested business books, go to www.ONOBook.com.

Twelve: It's All About Time Efficiency

"Don't say you don't have enough time. You have exactly the same number of hours per day that were given to Helen Keller, Pasteur, Michelangelo, Mother Teresa, Leonardo da Vinci, Thomas Jefferson, and Albert Einstein."

~ H. Jackson Brown, Jr.

Money is time, not the other way around. If you haven't already started making this mindset shift, do it now. From this moment onward, make a conscious decision to make the most money in the least amount of time. Don't work sloppily, or half-heartedly; work efficiently, because **money is time**.

Think about how much time you would have if you were more efficient. What would you do with that extra time? Probably whatever delicious thing you wanted to do.

The other day I was scheduling an appointment with an associate, and I told him that I needed two hours of his time later that week. He reminded me that it was Friday, and I said to myself, "Wow, where did the week go?"

I started thinking about my lost week, and I wondered how many of those weeks that seem to rush past so quickly do I have left in my lifetime. After some quick calculation, I realized that at my current age of 38, I only have 2080 weeks left. I then really punched myself in the gut when I did the math and realized that I only had 697 weeks left until my young son would probably be moving out of our home.

As a Family First Entrepreneur, those statistics scared me. I am flat out unwilling to use any of my precious time inefficiently while producing wealth. Not only that, I am also not going to spend money frivolously because of its impact on my time. You have to consider time as your most precious commodity. In order to realize the delicious benefits of ONO, you must get clear about what time means to you and how careful you need to be about giving it away.

Chore Time vs. Me Time

The seeds for the concept of what I now call ONO were planted very early in my life. I'm pretty sure that the idea of being in a place where I was free of obligations and could spend my time doing what I wanted began when I was three or four years old. My mom tells stories about me rushing through meals so I could go out and play, or so I could "fish" in my little plastic wading pool.

Later, when I was six, seven, and eight, I had chores to do. Some were daily chores like taking care of my pets, cleaning up my toys, things of that sort, and some were SATURDAY CHORES. I hated Saturday chores, especially the big one: cleaning my room. On Saturday, I had to have that room cleaned before I could do anything else.

Chores were my early obligations, and those obligations, especially the Saturday ones, taught me three valuable lessons. I learned that:

- Some were fun and some were not.
- Obligation time came before fun time.
- Any given chore could be done quickly or it could take a LONG time.

Like most kids back then, I loved to play and I loved to watch my favorite shows on TV. In fact, when I was in the first grade I'd get up at 5:30 *in the morning* to watch the Lone Ranger reruns. Of course, I didn't want to go to bed at night, either. I wanted to stay up and play some more, especially in the summer. There just never seemed to be enough time to do whatever I wanted, and having to do chores limited that time even more. I learned quickly that chores had to be done, no matter how much I didn't want to do them.

I also learned at that young age that the best way to budget my time, in order to make the most "me time" possible, was to get up and get my chores done the first thing in the morning and to get them finished quickly. I didn't know it then, but I created three rules for myself and I follow them to this day. They are *Marc's Three Rules of Time Efficiency*. Of course, they're not new rules. Your grandmother probably told you the same three things. They are:

- do it quickly,

- **do it well** (or you'll end up doing it all over again and that will cost you a whole lot more time), and

- **do it now**.

I learned and applied the first two principles easily. The last one, "do it now," was a huge struggle for me until I became sober. Procrastination is a trait that a lot of us share. It can be a real obstacle on the path to ONO.

The trick is to become result-focused. If it's a do it now or do it later situation, ask yourself, "Does doing this task now mean I will get to my goal more quickly, or can it wait because it won't make a difference?" If you need to do it now, do it now. And of course, do it well and do it quickly.

Short-Term Goals Create High Productivity

In high school and college, I was a huge homework-hater. It became almost as big a nemesis as my Saturday chores. I always preferred hunting, fishing, playing sports, or going out on dates. Really, I would rather have done just about anything than homework. Because of that, I put off homework obligations until the last minute.

It's not that I did not want to learn, in fact I longed for learning. The problem with school was that I wanted to learn experientially and most of my school experiences did not offer me that opportunity. I felt very confined by school. I didn't want to write reports and do big projects. I didn't find that those things were very valuable learning experiences. I felt that I would have learned so much more if the material had been presented in a more relevant, hands-on fashion.

Though I procrastinated in high school, when it came down to getting the work done, I worked very hard. I knew that I wanted to get into a great college that would eventually help me land a great job. I had visions of college as a place where I would learn true skills and earn the experience that would prepare me for the real world. However, when I finally got to college, I still felt like something was missing. I didn't feel my brain was being stretched enough. Even though I was busier with school, work, and sports, I put off doing my college homework even more than I had with high school. Most people would call that procrastinating, but back then, I called it *time efficiency*.

I read a great book recently called *The 4-Hour Work Week*, by Tim Ferriss. During a portion of the book, Ferriss talks about time efficiency and methods he has developed to make the most of his time. When I read that particular section, I felt like I was reading about myself. He talked about how good he was at putting things off. He would wait until the last minute to get projects and assignments done and still do reasonably well on them. What he paid attention to, and what I really want to tip my hat to, was that he found that short-term goals were very attainable. They created an immediacy and urgency that allowed for top-level performance.

I realized that this was why I had procrastinated in high school and college. When I was under the pressure of a time constraint, I had to perform efficiently in order to finish. A project that was supposed to take six weeks would take me eight hours.

The Denny's Zone

When I had a paper due or a test coming up, I would go into what I called my "Denny's Zone;" I'd go down to a Denny's restaurant late at night where I would be free of distraction. There I had all I needed: a table, 24-hour service, and a bottomless cup of coffee.

This was the way I wrote up projects, did reports and studied for tests. On the night before a major test, I would write my own practice test. I would literally stay up all night at Denny's and think of all the possible questions that might be on the test, using my lecture notes and the textbooks. Most of these pre-tests I built had four to six hundred questions. I would then memorize my test. I basically crammed all of the information into my head at night and then spat it all out the next day. I found that I could consistently score in the high-B, low-A range with this method. That was good enough for me. When it came to the final exams, I struggled a bit because my retention rate was poor, but my method worked well for me in the short term.

Now, I'm not suggesting that you do this because my long-term retention wasn't very good, but I got the one thing I knew I needed— good grades. I knew I needed good grades to get that diploma, that piece of paper, and I spent the least amount of time possible to get it. However, my college system of *working at very high levels for short-term* performance was a good one in terms of **time efficiency.** It doesn't apply in every situation, but it's something to consider.

Set goals and set short-term activity periods in which to accomplish those goals. Ferriss' advice is never to set a task goal for longer than 72 hours. I agree with him. I have found, however, that 24 to 48 hours is even better. If I can break a task down to a 24 to 48 hour time span, complete it and then move on to the next one, it creates an enormous amount of efficiency in my business. I encourage you to try it.

Systems of Efficiency

During my college years, I took my efficiency methods with me from school to the workplace. I worked part time as a waiter in a little Mexican restaurant. I developed my own system to maximize the return on my time investment on the job.

As everyone knows, the way to make money as a waiter is through tips. I studied my customers and tested different serving styles to find ways to earn the best tips. I then began taking note of the regulars and noticed how they wanted to be treated, remembering which items they ordered and watching for any idiosyncrasies that set them apart from other customers. When I served regulars, I would cater to their preferences without having to be asked. I learned their names and made sure they remembered mine.

I soon learned every regular's tipping style. I found out who tipped well and who didn't. I made sure to give extra special attention to those who tipped well, and because of that, they would ask to sit in my section every time they came in.

In my brief time at that restaurant, besides maximizing my earning efforts, I learned a lot about how to run a business. I paid attention to the little things that distinguished successful and not-so-successful businesses from one another.

My next business effort taught me even more about entrepreneurism. During college summer breaks, I painted house numbers on street curbs. I worked with a partner and learned about some of the complications that can come up within a business partnership. I also got a taste of *my ability to earn good money.* That's when things started to open up for me. Granted, I was still trading far too much time and effort for that money, but I was learning.

In fact, I determined that my learning experience on the job was so much more valuable to me than my time in the classroom that I decided to quit college. I knew the entrepreneurial road was for me. I felt there was nothing I was going to learn at school that I couldn't learn better from business mentors or my own experiences. I have never looked back.

Let me get back to my original point. Develop systems that maximize your efficiency in your place of work and which optimize making money, money that you exchange for the time you give up. Always be aware of the results of your actions. Making every action an efficient one will move you further down the path and closer to ONO.

It's All About Time Efficiency

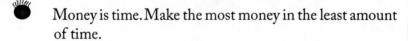

- Money is time. Make the most money in the least amount of time.

- Setting short-term goals will keep you productive and will save you time.

- Create systems that allow you to be time efficient.

- Be proactive in creating your own wealth.

Thirteen: The Money Factor

No one is born with the idea of financial normalcy.
It is something that has to be learned.

I was raised in a household where there was never enough money. Mom was a beginning teacher and a single parent for a while. Back then as now, teachers were paid peanuts. She worked two jobs for twenty years just to make ends meet for our family. To complicate things, soon after she married the man who adopted me, he got cancer. Thank God Dad survived it, and thank God we had insurance.

The medical costs were huge, even after insurance, and Dad couldn't work for a year, so it took quite awhile to get our finances back in order. During this time, there was no extra money. My sister and I had to rely on ourselves to earn money for entertainment and extra clothes. I began to see that there was a definite difference between the things I needed and the things I wanted.

Because our family situation was so tight financially, I began my working life when I was nine. I worked on Saturdays for a veterinarian cleaning out stalls and cages. I also raised steers. My dad worked for a farmer, and we had a couple of pastures next to the house. I bought three dairy calves at the local auction, and I bottle fed them until they were able to eat grass. When they became 250-pound steers, I took them back and sold them at the same auction. I was pretty decent at saving my money and by the time I got my driver's license at fourteen, I had already purchased my first car, a Datsun 240Z. It was a cool car for a ninth grader, and it was my pride and joy.

During those early years, I made a conscious decision that someday I was going to have *enough money to buy whatever I needed and whatever I wanted.* In high school and college, my feelings about trading time for money intensified. I wanted a lot of money and I wanted to spend the least amount of time earning it. I began to seek jobs that offered the most money for the time expended. I was a crew boss for a crop-dusting crew—good money. I became the co-owner of a curb painting business—great money. Then at age twenty-two, I ended up in Wyoming working for NFIB because it paid the most money I could make for the time I put into it. This focus, making more and more money in less and less time has continued to this day.

More than Money

It was also in Wyoming that I realized that there was more to life than having a lot of money. I was making darned good pay, but I began to see that there were other things in life that were important, too. In addition, God became a much bigger player in my life. The houses of Amway and Alcoholics Anonymous were huge influences. The books, tapes, and AA meetings fed my mind with spiritual and self-growth messages and I became very committed to change.

While working for the National Federation of Independent Businesses, I got a good look at all sorts of successful businesses, both large and small: ranches, law firms, bars, manufacturing facilities, construction companies, restaurants, banks, and so forth. When I talked to the men and women who owned these businesses, my sensory receptors flared and my natural curiosity was supercharged. I wanted to know about their success or lack of it, about the money they made or didn't, about their core beliefs—business as well as spiritual—and about all the details of running their businesses. I paid attention and gathered information, some directly, some indirectly. My sales and renewal presentations became conversational and the conversations allowed me to add to my spiritual and business wisdom. I moved back to Boise and eventually left NFIB for another opportunity that gave me a chance to make more money and spend less time doing it.

Enter Sue

Then, a personal opportunity presented itself. I met and married Sue—**Higher Purpose, Part One**. I promised her on our wedding day that I would be there for her and for our marriage. I would be a committed husband. When Sue and I teamed up, we went from making terrific money to making awesome money, but our lives were very hectic. We traveled and worked all the time. We knew that we were sacrificing many of the things we wanted in our lives, but our goal was to build a substantial investment fund (what I now call an ONO account), and we had the opportunity to work side by side. Then Jaken was born—**Higher Purpose, Part Two**.

While Sue was pregnant, my friends and family all laughed at me because of the naïve expectations I had about being a parent. I figured we would work just as hard and continue doing what we were doing after Jaken was born. After all, he was going to be a baby, right? We would just take him along with us, no problem. In fact, three months before he was born, I scheduled us for another full work year—254 days of work on the road.

Wrong move Marc. When Jaken was two hours old, I *thought* maybe I had made a mistake with the big schedule.

When he was two weeks old, I *knew* I had made a mistake. I wanted to be a hands-on dad. I didn't want to miss out on the opportunity to raise my son. I knew then that for the rest of my working life my family would come first. My evolution from an entrepreneur to a Family First Entrepreneur began.

Sue and I were blessed with another son in November 2007. Tucker reinforced every decision and sacrifice I had made to have more time to spend being a father.

Finding Financial Normalcy

As grownups, we are all long past the days of worrying about nothing more serious than which toy to play with next. We are now adults, but many of us still have not learned the lessons of financial responsibility, and along with adulthood come many expectations and responsibilities, whether we are prepared for them or not.

We are all expected to live the American dream. We are expected to get good jobs and to take on the responsibilities of our occupations. We are expected to provide for our families financially, and at the same time, we are supposed to spend quality time being good spouses and good parents. We are also expected to prepare for retirement. The problem is that many of us feel the pressure of these expectations and responsibilities, but we really have no idea how to prepare for them. No one is born with the idea of financial normalcy. It is something that has to be learned.

The Generational Perspective

When my grandparents were kids, the Great Depression was in full swing. They were raised with a very narrow view of money. Don't spend it. Be frugal. They also had a dim view of wealth and wealthy people. They believed that if you didn't work your fingers to the bone to earn your money, then you didn't deserve it. If you wanted more money, you worked harder. They looked down on people who "came into easy money."

Frugality is great, but the mistake my grandparents made was stuffing the money they saved under their mattresses or burying it in the back yard as opposed to investing it to amplify its growth. Investments implied a certain amount of risk to my grandparents, but putting it at no risk was not necessarily the appropriate choice. Still, our grandparents were a great example to us about saving money, and as we have already seen, saving money is a stepping-stone to reaching ONO.

The children of the people who lived through the Great Depression were the Baby Boomers. Baby Boomers like my parents believed that hard work brought lifestyle and lifestyle was something that all Americans deserved, whether it was affordable or not. Credit became the new vehicle to get what they "deserved." Of course, they also believed that the only other way to get more money was to work harder. People in my parents' generation viewed wealthy people as either lucky or crooked, but they also thought that all people were entitled to an affluent lifestyle.

Sadly, because of inflation, lifestyle for the people in my generation costs so much more than it did in our parents' day. We are a society that's living on champagne when we can only afford beer. Lifestyle is so expensive today that we don't even have the option to use credit any more. To make things worse, there is massive competition for what I like to call the lifestyle dollar.

On the bright side, our attitudes about work and earning have shifted generationally from working harder to working smarter. People are more aware of how they spend their time and energy. They want to be more efficient. They want to earn more and to expend less time and energy doing it. They are thinking about what they can and want to do with their free time, and they want more of it.

Success is an Attitude

In summary, while it is valuable to gain a generational perspective about attitudes toward work and toward money, it's more about choosing your own attitudes and beliefs. This book is about getting rid of the attitudes and belief systems that haven't been serving you. For one thing, if you think that the only way you can make honest money is by having sweat roll off your brow, then you're lying to yourself. More importantly, if you think you can buy lifestyle on credit without digging yourself into a huge hole, you're mistaken. Look around. You'll see people who are on the edge of bankruptcy. They spent every bit of their money and credit on lifestyle.

I am around people all the time who are going down this road to "success," or at least they have the appearance of being successful. Most of these people make much less than I do, yet they appear to be far better off. They have nicer cars, nicer clothes, nicer homes, and nicer jewelry, but they have no buffer fund, no savings, and little or no money in investments. They live day to day, money-in, money-out, and paycheck-to-paycheck. They are drowning in debt. These are the impersonators of successful people.

The American dream should be defined in terms of true financial security, but many American people define wealth and success in terms of material possessions (owned or financed). They think it means living with your beautiful spouse, on a hill with a beautiful view, in a big house full of beautiful possessions, and of course, driving a new car. This mindset is a flawed one, and many people pretend to live the dream but cannot afford it.

True success is defined by the serenity of your lifestyle. It means being comfortable in body, mind, and spirit. You do not desperately trade a lot of your time for money to keep your financial head above water. The possessions you own are paid for. You are debt-free. Creating success is a process that takes work, but when done right, you will be greatly rewarded in the end. You cannot expect real success to come from the newest and best material wants, especially early in your growth process. Truly successful people have options, not obligations in terms of both their time and their money.

"Strawberries—Two Dollars!"

It took a long time for me to really understand the nature of wealth and the importance of financial responsibility. As a father and a Family First Entrepreneur, I did not want my sons to have the same hurdles to jump. I vowed, even before they were born, to teach them how to handle money and have a true appreciation for it. This is the story of Jaken's first entrepreneurial experience and his introduction to financial responsibility.

The story began when Jaken and I were looking through a catalog one day and he spotted a toy he really wanted. He asked me, "Daddy, can I please have that?" He had a basement full of toys at the time, and the last thing he needed was another one to add to the collection, so I told him, "You have lots of toys, and I don't really want to buy you another one right now." That was when it hit me; this would be a great opportunity for me to teach my son about how to earn money. So I said, "I will not buy you that toy, but I will help you make some money so that you can buy it for yourself." His face lit up.

We have a giant organic strawberry patch in our garden. It produces more strawberries in one day than my family can eat in a week. I decided that a fun and easy way to make some money with Jaken would be to pick little bags of strawberries, set up a stand outside our house, and then sell them to people in our neighborhood. We started picking and soon had a table full of bags. We made signs that said, "Jaken's Organic Strawberries." Organic strawberries are usually expensive, but I had no intention of making a large profit, I just wanted Jaken to have a successful experience, so we priced each bag at only two dollars.

We live in a subdivision where almost everybody has to drive by my house in order to get to theirs, so we had a perfect spot to set up. Cars started coming by shortly after five, and I had Jaken in position. I had him wave to make sure he got people's attention as they passed by. So there he was, a three-year-old sitting at a little table, waving and smiling at every car that drove by.

It was a successful venture. People couldn't resist Jaken and his smile. They couldn't turn around fast enough to come back and buy his strawberries. It was crazy, complete with screeching tires. When people approached the table, Jaken was so nervous that all he could say was, "They're two dollars. It's two dollars." He couldn't find any more words than that.

They'd pay him, and with utter delight, he'd quietly smile and tuck the money away. We counted his money as we were going along so he could really get a grasp of the "wealth" he was accumulating.

In the first 35 or 40 minutes, there were times when we had people actually waiting in line. We soon ran out of full bags, so I ran up to the garden and started picking strawberries as fast as I could in order to get him more. I had no idea it would go as well as it did.

Teaching Responsibility

After the flurry was over and we were out of strawberries, I sat him down and told him about the responsibility and duty that comes with having money. I explained to him that this money, as well as any other money that he made in the future, would be split into three different accounts (or in his case, piggybanks). I told him that he was allowed to do whatever he wanted with 70 percent of his earnings. Guess what we went shopping for that next day? Yep, that toy. Of the remaining 30 percent, 20 percent would go into a savings account, and 10 percent would be given to a charity of his choice.

I explained what these things meant. I broke down the concept of saving and investing into three year-old language. Trust me, it's harder than it sounds. I also told him what it meant to donate money to a charity and at the same time attempted to explain the value of time. I told him that people in need can be helped by both the gift of money and the gift of time, that giving time is often as valuable, if not more valuable, than giving money.

Jaken learned some awesome lessons that day: lessons about hard work and running a business, about making money, and most importantly, about how to handle money unselfishly and responsibly. Entrepreneurism is a great concept to teach children when they are young. It is one of the greatest gifts you can ever give them. There are many other fun ideas for teaching your children about how to make and handle money on my website, www.ONOBook.com.

Your Magic Number

Life is about being with your family, not about pursuing wealth. Life is about watching the sun come up on a new day, a day you get to spend making a difference, a day with opportunities to play, to learn, to love. Life is about the relationship between you and your spouse and your kids, wherein you spend the time necessary to create quality relationships, and you have the energy to commit to them. However, if a large amount of your time is spent pursuing money to meet your obligations, then there is very little time left to enjoy the delicious things in life.

ONO is about not having to serve money; it is about money serving you. When you reach ONO, you can step away knowing that all your financial needs are taken care of. That's what ONO is all about; it's about getting to that point and, of course, enjoying the journey it takes to get there.

Really, everything about being a human is a journey. We go through life, we evolve, and we travel down a winding path to an unknown destination. We're going to be on this journey for the rest of our lives and we'll go through lots of different processes. It makes it hard to see where we are when we don't know the final destination because it's always changing and evolving. That is normal for most of the aspects of life's journey—we don't really have a clear picture of our destination.

I have good news about our financial journey, though. *Financially, there can be a clearly defined destination.* We can see it and we can make plans to get there. I call it a "magic number."

Your magic number is a specific amount of money that you have in cash-flowing investments that produces enough income for you to be free from financial burdens.

Your magic number is your financial destination number. It is the amount of income sufficient to provide for all your needs and all the wants that you decide are important to you.

Just as I had you determine your Higher Purpose by writing out a eulogy, I now want you to take your first step toward creating financial freedom. Figure out your magic number. That number is the amount of money that you need in order to live a life free of obligations. It is at the end of your path. In essence, it is ONO.

1) Set a *target age*. Your magic number will be a whole lot different if you're twenty-five now and you want to be at ONO when you're forty than if you are thirty-five now and want to be at ONO by the time you're forty-five. Let's say you're sixty, retired, and own your own house. You could be at ONO almost immediately. Achieving that may simply involve creating a way for your equity money to provide a little additional income for you.

2) Calculate your magic number, the dollar amount of income you will need each month to meet your obligations, both your wants and your needs, *when you get to your target age.* I also want you to assume that your house and your cars will be paid for by that time. Getting to ONO will include strategies to pay off both. So, with all debt aside, how much money would you need on a monthly basis to

live comfortably and to fulfill your Higher Purpose? To make this exercise easier, use the worksheets you'll find at www.ONObook. com. They will do most of the calculations for you.

Wants vs. Needs Revisited

You've already done some of the hard part; you've placed your wants and needs in categories, so start with your needs. What do you *need* every month to live comfortably? Don't list your house and vehicles; remember, they'll be paid off by then. Identify your monthly needs: food, insurance, utilities, fuel, etc. Get a rough estimate of how much money it would take to cover those things every month when you are at your targeted ONO age. Figure in an inflation rate of three percent per year.

Your wants are a completely different animal. As I said before, we live in a materialistic world where your level of success is often judged in terms of your material possessions. I hope that by now, your mindset has changed and you've created a new definition of wealth for yourself.

Wealth is not about dropping your child off at school in your brand new BMW and then heading off to your eight-to-five job so you can make money to afford the payments; it is about taking your child to school in the three-year-old minivan that you own outright. Then, instead of going to work, you have the freedom to stay and go with your son or daughter on a class field trip because you are in a position where you are in control of your own time. When you are at ONO, you will be living the life you want to live.

Next, figure out what your *wants* are going to be when you reach ONO. Your Higher Purpose will come into play here as well. Let's say you want to spend a year away from home doing mission work for your church or some other organization. You'd probably factor in some cost figures for that. Maybe you want to go back to school; there are also cost implications to that kind of a Higher Purpose. Most of our Higher Purpose activities, even speaking to seventh graders in your community about survival skills or collecting food bank donations, have cost implications. Factor in those costs.

Once your wants are determined, add the cost of them together, add that to your needs number, and you will have determined what it is going to take to live comfortably every month. Multiply that number by twelve and you will have your yearly income goal.

(Monthly Needs + Monthly Wants + ONO Account) x 12 months =

Future Yearly Income Needed To Be At ONO

(Multiply your final number by three percent every year to allow for inflation)

You now have a pretty clear picture of your magic number. Are you a little intimidated by it? Remember the rushing river? You're on one side; the place called ONO is on the other. Actually, you have moved since we last talked about the river. You've taken a giant leap and landed on the first stepping-stone. Figuring out your magic number is one of the first steps—and it's a big one.

Great! Now what? *Now you think like an entrepreneur.* You make a plan to produce income to meet that number without working another forty or fifty hours a week for thirty years.

Part of your income-producing plan is probably in place. You may have stock market investments, which have been producing income for you for some time, or you may own rentals or other real estate properties. You may have a chunk of land that you purchased and developed; you may decide to sell it, invest the money, and produce income. If you wanted to wait that long, income could come from tax-sheltered annuities. Just as long as you have enough in combined investments and liquid assets to give you the income you need to lead the ONO lifestyle, you're there.

There is no one single way to reach that magic number. There is no limit to the opportunities that are out there for you; you just have to be creative.

ONO Plans

There are many ways to get to your magic number. Here are a few:

- I know a man who bought a patch of dirt on the outskirts of town. He worked at his job for thirty years and made the payments on it. He sold the land, invested the money, and the return on his investments provides him with his magic number figure. He retired; he is in that delicious place called ONO. He is set for the rest of his life.

- My friend Huck got there by setting up enhancements to his retirement plan. Do you know that if you only bought one rental property every three years, at the end of thirty years you'd have ten rentals? A conservative figure for the value of those assets would be one to two million dollars in today's market.

- Of course, if you just put $2,000 into a conservative investment, say one that earned five percent a year when you were twenty years old, and you added $2,000 each year to that figure, by the time you were thirty-five, it would be worth $48,000. That's a tidy sum of money to use to invest in more entrepreneurial, higher-yield vehicles that have the potential of earning you twelve to fifteen percent.

- There are plenty of people who use capital gains exemptions on their personal residences as investment vehicles. Buy a house; live in it for two years. When you sell it, your profit is tax-free money. Did you hear that? Tax-free money. Do that every two years. Buy the houses at the right price, maybe do a little work on them, earn a little sweat equity, and you'll have some serious money in ten years.

How will you build your wealth? You will make surplus money *by not spending all your money on wants.* You will figure out what you really need. You will be frugal; you will spend money on needs, and when you start down the path to wealth, you will spend very little money on wants. You will be determined to build your wealth by sacrificing immediate wants for long-term gain.

Deals on Wheels

When Sue and I were working to build our ONO account, we were spending way more time on the road than we did at home. Home for us was a hotel room. It got really old, really fast.

Long before I met Sue, I had learned that there was a direct correlation between my comfort level and my performance level. Now, I'm not talking about the lap of luxury, I'm talking about a good night's sleep, healthy food, privacy—those sorts of things. I would tell Sue, "My personal comfort level makes us money." Staying in hotels when we were on the road was a huge energy drain for me. The added stress of having to find a room and then move our stuff in and out after a hard day's work was limiting my productivity. I couldn't show up ready to do what I had to do to the best of my ability. I needed a change.

So we bought a motor home. I could sleep in my own bed, and prepare and eat my own healthy food. I could be at "home" on the road. Even though we bought a used one, it still cost quite a bit, so I ran the decision through my filters. I did the math before we bought it and realized that it would more than pay for itself. The combination of added comfort, eating in, and the tax benefits (including depreciation) actually made us money.

Measure Your Actions

When unsure about making decisions of this nature, run the numbers. It keeps you logical. ***Spend money only when it makes you money.*** You're going to have many opportunities to spend money, especially when you start having a surplus, like buying a car, buying a new house, buying healthy food, eating out at restaurants, starting a business venture, or making investments. Every opportunity, every choice, has the potential to either take you off the path or further down the path.

With every financial or business decision on your path to ONO, measure the results of your actions. Ask, "Will this be productive and help me move down the path toward my goal?" Make sure the money and time you spend are not taking you off on a tangent or being wasted. Both time and money at this point in the game are available to you in limited quantities. Remember, between age 20 and age 70, you have only 2,600 weeks. What are you doing with every precious week? You need to be conscious of that.

One excellent filter is your Higher Purpose. By defining my Higher Purpose, I could evaluate the urge, the opportunity, whatever it was, to spend money or to make money, and ask, "Does that move me further along the path or does it distract me from it? Does it take me away from what I really want?" Do you see how these questions are like a filter system? You will be able to take each opportunity and to evaluate it as it comes up. Run it through your filters. Ask yourself, "Does it take me away from what I really want, or does it move me toward my goal?"

~ *Opportunity for Reflection* ~

Now that you have an idea of what you want out of life, list some changes you could make to get your family further down the path to ONO.

_____

_____

_____

_____

The Money Factor

- Money is important, but there is so much more to life than money.

- Parents have the duty to provide an example of responsible money management for their children.

- ONO is about not having to serve money; it's about having money serve you.

- Identify your magic number. Reaching this number will set you free.

- Run every decision through your filters. Make sure each decision is building your wealth.

Fourteen: Operating From a Spirit of Generosity

Treating everyone with kindness and respect is not only the right thing to do; it's the smart thing to do.

Several years ago, I had the opportunity to hear Mark Victor Hansen speak. Hansen is the co-creator of *Chicken Soup for the Soul* and *The One Minute Millionaire*. I loved the jovial, easy, free-of-limitations way he spoke. I could tell that he was telling his story just because he loved telling his story. It was a presentation of his general business philosophy, but he was having a great time with it.

Hansen is a man of great fame and fortune. He has made some very smart business moves and has created a great deal of wealth. But what inspired me most about him was not how he *acquired* his wealth, but the way he *uses* his wealth. Mark Victor Hansen is a philanthropic entrepreneur. He invests in people.

The Philanthropic Entrepreneur

An example of Hansen's type of philanthropy would look something like this: You go into a South American village and invest a large sum of money to build some sort of business, like a coffee plantation. That plantation then creates jobs and income for the local economy. You use your money to give people a leg up, in this case, a whole village of people. You create ways for the people to be successful financially. It's great.

What's greater is that it completes the circle: you invest money, the people you invest in make money, they spend money, and the village's economy gets a large boost. It doesn't stop there. Not only are the people in the village making money, you make money from your investment, and with those profits, you have the capacity to start another philanthropic venture in a new area. You don't give handouts; you give "hand-ups."

Mark Victor Hansen's speech was the spark that triggered my belief about the finer aspects of wealth and wealthy people. It's what I call the spirit of generosity. **The spirit of generosity is doing business from a place of help or service first and a place of profit second.** It does not mean we need to give things away or feel guilty for charging for products and services. It's purely a mindset; it's a spirit that should be pervasive in our business dealings. We look to help first, and we know all the rest, including revenue, will follow.

Full Circle

One of the keys to success in the pursuit of ONO is understanding the principle of operating from a spirit of generosity as opposed to a spirit of greed. This means doing business with the intent of lifting up and fulfilling others through your actions.

Does this mean that you operate at a loss? Absolutely not. You are in business, after all, but every business deal you put together should be structured so that *both parties benefit*. It's a smart move business-wise.

Give-and-take comes with operating from this mindset. It's not about expecting others to reciprocate either, it just happens. Help me, and I help you. What goes around comes around. Make money, spend money, then others make money. I pay it forward, you pay it forward. It's a big circle.

The full circle, the what-goes-around-comes-around concept, is present in all our behaviors and interactions. If I'm operating from the spirit of greed to get self-fulfillment in business, those actions will not go unnoticed.

When your business is operated from a spirit of greed, the short-term rewards may be great, but it will always come back to bite you in the long run. When we operate from a spirit of generosity instead of greed, we try to help our clients, to give them the best service at the best price, to make an impact, and then, *we use a portion of the profit to make a difference for other people.* It's important to align your business practices with your spiritual beliefs because when you're not operating from a spirit of generosity, you tend to make poor choices.

The Endpoint

Instead of looking for a starting point at the beginning a business relationship, I think about an endpoint. What do I want to get out of this business deal, and what are the other parties involved going to receive? Do I want a continued relationship with this person? What do I need to do now to ensure that? How can I ensure that we both benefit?

In my daily lifestyle, I give of myself freely. I give my love, my compassion, my support, a smile, a hello, or whatever. I believe that if I do that, then it is going to go out, multiply, and find its way back to me. I believe doing right in business is the same as doing right in the world; it is a reflection of our spiritual side, the better, higher part of us. I know that operating generously does not limit my business. In fact, that generosity goes out and multiplies and eventually comes back to reward my business tenfold. I believe this is a spiritual law of business.

The Foreclosure Story

I have many examples of times when I have seen generosity come full circle to benefit my businesses and me. One of my favorite examples is the story of how I acquired one of my rental properties.

I had heard about an investment property, a small house for sale that might work well as a rental. I followed up on the lead, went to look at the house, and met the owner. She was a single mother who was going through some tough times. She was only three days away from foreclosure. She had already gotten all the paperwork together.

The sheriff was going to show up and kick her out, the whole nine yards.

I visited with this woman for quite a long time. She was a sweet lady doing everything she could to provide for herself and four kids. One of her two jobs had just been outsourced and everything seemed to be caving in on her at the same time. She seemed very fragile to me; she was at the end of her rope and in a very vulnerable position. Someone operating from the spirit of greed could have easily taken advantage of her. I was glad she was talking to me because I really felt for her, and I knew I could help her. She had put herself in a situation that limited what I could do for her, but I knew I could do something.

Discussion vs. Negotiation

In my business life, I prefer to discuss as opposed to negotiate, and this situation definitely called for this approach. After some friendly discussion, we got into the figures. The house was worth about $140,000. In previous discussions with her, my scout had found out that she was hoping to get something in the $115,000 range. I knew she was backed so far into a corner that I could have gotten her to drop that number considerably. However, my goal was to get a good deal and, at the same time, make sure that her family was taken care of.

So I built a relationship with her. I befriended her. I told her about my business reputation, that I was a moral and ethical man, that both my spirituality and my relationship with others were very important to me in business. She disclosed that she owed $98,000 on the house. She opened up to me and trusted me. I had faith in her as well, so I said to her, "All I need to know is a number. Tell me what you feel that you need. I want to make sure you and your family walk away with enough money to rebuild yourselves." We discussed her needs, and we talked about my need to make wise business decisions for my family. We agreed that a price of $115,000 would benefit everyone involved; we created what I call a give/give situation.

A Give-Give Solution

My next concern was the foreclosure and how long it would take her to vacate the house once I purchased it. So again, we sat down as two real people with mutual interests. We both were concerned for her family, and we both were well aware of the fact that this was still a business deal and that I had a responsibility to support my family by adhering to wise business principles.

She needed to live in the house for another month to give her time to find a new place. That was going to be inconvenient for me, because I had already had a renter for the house lined up, but I believe that what goes around, comes around, so I told her that she was welcome to live in the place for 30 days rent-free. However, I was clear about the fact that if she needed to live in it longer than 30 days, then I'd need to charge her rent, so I was able to be true to my business principles and also deal with her from a spirit of generosity.

The most urgent problem was that if she didn't write a check to her bank in three days, the foreclosure would begin, and then we would be in a completely different scenario. I wrote her a check on the spot and paid her mortgage and late fees. I told her that my check would be my receipt, and we wrote a short contract right there to cover the rest of the money details.

She walked away from that deal with $17,000 in cash, giving her the opportunity to get a fresh start with her credit rating still intact. I walked away from that deal feeling that I had done well business-wise, and more importantly, I had done the right and generous thing. There were tears. She cried a lot, hugged me, and then I teared up. It was a wonderful experience for me; it felt great.

Golden Rule

The Golden Rule of life is also the Golden Rule of business: *Do unto others, as you would have them do unto you.* Treat others the way you would want to be treated. It's just another aspect of operating out of the spirit of generosity, and it applies no matter which side of a transaction you're on.

Some people think that their behavior changes with the role they play. Because you are a customer, all of a sudden you have a right to be assertive, to be demanding, or even be a jerk. Assertive is fine, but it's also your *responsibility* to be the customer that you would want to have. Be a pleasure to deal with.

I see this as one of the core requirements of being able to achieve long-term success. It's a logical thing, and it's spiritual. My spiritual sense tells me that if I take care of other people, if I do what's right, and if I am a walking example of goodwill, love, and generosity, then I will be rewarded. Logic also tells me that being good to others is good business for me.

I had to learn this code of conduct, like many others in my life, the hard way. Early in my entrepreneurial career, I was willing to do whatever it took to make sure I was getting the best deal for my money. I became a ruthless negotiator. No matter where I went, I was "doing business." My wife hated to go anywhere with me. I would negotiate at Wal-Mart; I would negotiate everywhere we went for everything that we purchased, and I became really good at it. I got what I wanted.

This strategy worked very well for meeting my short-term needs, but I learned that my demanding actions weren't serving me in the end. I eventually destroyed many of my business relationships. I took advantage of people, I got more out of them than they got from me, and those people really didn't want to do business with me again. They would see me coming and say, "Oh no, here comes Marc again, he's going to work me over like an eight-hour shift," and they would avoid me.

It took a while, but I eventually learned that business was all about creating what I call a "give/give" situation. I like that term, because I don't think the term "win/win" goes far enough. It doesn't cover the idea of generosity that is so critical to doing business the ONO way. We should go beyond what is fair.

Many people in the business world don't understand that what's right to do is also what's smart to do. Take care of others and you will be taken care of. In business, what is moral and ethical is the way to success. The key to creating real success in business is building and relying on solid business relationships. Instead of taking advantage of others, you need to take care of others and, in return, they will take care of you.

Before I ever make a business deal with someone, I clearly outline what my expectations are, as well as what I think he or she will get from me in return. I ask people to give their best and I promise to do the same. I don't promise things that I'm not willing to do. If somebody does well on my behalf, I'm going to keep going back to that person because I know he or she will take care of me. Giving your best and delivering on your promises will create strong relationships that will serve you throughout your business career.

Respect

I'd like to add one more thought to your growing bank of ONO ideas. It is important to be respectful to everyone involved in the workplace or the transaction, not just the people with whom you're doing business directly. George Crile's book *Charlie Wilson's War* illustrates this principle well.

The character Gust Avrakotos was a major player in the CIA in the 1980's. Though he had some major character flaws, he knew how to treat people who could potentially benefit him in the future. Gust came off as obscene and abrasive to many people, but he treated the lower-level employees of the agency like gold. He took special care of the clerks, mail carriers, and secretaries. The CIA is a very secretive place and nothing that goes on within its walls is public knowledge. Gust used his connections with the lower level employees to find out classified information, and in the end, the fact that Gust took care of those people made all the difference in world for him.

Because of this, Gust became a very powerful presence. The point is to treat all people involved in your business life very well, because you never know who might make that huge difference for you when you need it. Treating *everyone* with kindness and respect is not only the right thing to do; it's the smart thing to do.

Build Relationships

One of the best ways to strengthen a business relationship is through referrals. When you are treated well in a business deal, one way to reciprocate is to patronize that person's business in the future. Another way to reciprocate is to send other business deals to them. Doing this creates a give/give situation for both involved parties. Remember, it is about "you give, I give."

Another benefit that often accompanies referrals is that you can create shortcuts based on mutual business relationships. You know someone who knows someone. If I trust a person, then you know you can trust him or her. Those shortcuts are especially helpful when you are under time constraints or when you need to cut to the chase in a business transaction.

Tipping

As I told you before, earlier in my entrepreneurial career I was in a "you give/I take" business mindset, but it didn't take me long to see the error in that sort of thinking. I now operate from a spirit of gratitude and generosity. I now know the importance of a give/give business exchange. In fact, I now try to go beyond give/give. When I make money from someone else's efforts, I always tip that person. Now, that's not common in business. For example, let's say somebody tells me about a house that is looking a little run down, but seems to have a lot of potential. If, after careful consideration, I buy that house, I then give the person who found the deal for me a generous tip.

There is a flipside benefit to tipping. Although I have no expectations, what often ends up happening is that the person is going to pass on helpful information to me next time, too. You help me; I give you a gift of gratitude. It is as simple as that. When I make money, I make sure that the people who helped me do it get something in return. One of the neater parts for me in the giving of gifts is that it's not just about money; it's about gratitude and relationship, therefore my tips are often not in the form of money. Remember the foreclosure story? An associate of mine found that property and did the initial research on it for me. As a tip for his referral, I bought him the $1,000 hunting bow he had been wanting.

Broken Trust

Of course, there is always risk. Not every good faith gesture turns out as intended. One of my strong early business relationships turned out to be an example of the opposite kind of business relationship, one that went sour. I had a business partner, a man I trusted with my personal deals, and to whom I had referred $15 million in business over a period of several years.

I did business with him even though he was more expensive than others in his industry were, because I believed he would step up to the plate for me. I would rather have him making money from my business than somebody I didn't know who offered a better deal. We had developed a relationship where I would do anything I could to help him, and he would do the same for me, or so I thought. Unfortunately, he ended up taking advantage of my situation, putting my family in a position where we had to search urgently for new financial options. It was a big blow for us, and it was the last time I ever did business with him.

Do I regret building that relationship and putting my trust in him? No, I don't. Building and maintaining strong business relationships will serve you more often than not, but they are not fail-proof. The chances of a trusted business partner backing you into a corner are far less likely than a person about whom you know nothing. Building these relationships and doing business with trusted colleagues minimizes your risk but cannot eliminate it.

Building Safety Nets

Over the last fifteen years, I have put myself in a position through my business relationships where, if I ever do become a little financially vulnerable and need help, I have people on whom I can rely. I have safety nets. I can fall back on those safety nets for financial stability if necessary. While having true Options not Obligations is about not needing safety nets, during your journey to ONO, these safety nets are important.

In your early entrepreneurial days, when you are doing everything you can to build wealth, you spend a lot of time bridging one deal into the next. For me, there were periods when my ONO account was depleted and I had to reposition myself by means of short-term loans. Because those loans came from people that I had previously helped to make a lot of money and because I had relationships built on trust prior to my needing their help, it was easy for me to ask for help and for them to offer it.

Those people didn't mind stepping up and saying, "You know what Marc? I trust you. I believe in you. Yeah, I can put $100,000 in your account for a month and I know you're good for it." There was no extensive paperwork. We wrote up a quick IOU and we shook hands. It was old-school business, the kind of thing that can only happen when you have an established relationship.

It is important to develop a network of people in each area of your business and personal life. Every one of us needs and wants guidance. In turn, others need us. If you don't have a network of key people around you from whom you receive guidance and support and to whom you give guidance and support, then you are missing a big part of the picture. Operate out of the spirit of generosity, give of yourself, and show that you are willing to give without any strings attached. Then, of course, the natural cycle takes over, and you receive tenfold in return.

Operating from a Spirit of Generosity

- Greed may appear to serve you in the present, but it will undermine you in the end.

- Before you enter any business transaction, ask yourself, "Am I going to be making a difference for others as well as for myself?"

- Every deal you make should benefit all of the parties involved; create *give/give* situations.

- Treat others the way you want to be treated. Uphold this principle in business, as well as in all aspects of your life.

- Actively refer clients to people with whom you do business.

Fifteen: Ready...Aim...Fire!

It's time to put your thought processes into action.

Throughout the first section of the book, we've been discussing "how to think." This next section is more directly applicable to your first or your next entrepreneurial venture. This is where you put your thought processes into action.

Entrepreneurism can be defined as a series of "good guesses." For those of you who are scared away by the word "guess," let's call them "educated decisions."

The reality of business is that there are no crystal balls, but every business has a winning formula that you can learn. To be a successful businessperson, become a good accumulator of information, and base your business decisions on that acquired knowledge. Learn your industry. Through that knowledge and wisdom, you predict future trends and changes and then draw conclusions and strategies from your predictions.

This process is what I call the "**Ready...Aim...Fire**" theory of business. In the next three sections, I will walk you methodically through Ready, Aim, and Fire and show you how to use this process to create good guesses of your own.

The Process

All good decision makers go through a detailed process that allows them to check for potential roadblocks and make solid choices. The first step, "Ready," is simply identifying what you want, looking for and being ready for an opportunity when it presents itself, and making sure that you are physically and mentally prepared to take action.

When you are ready to take action, the next step is to "Aim" at an appropriate target, taking into account both direction and timing. Aiming is gathering the necessary information needed to make that decision; it's the due diligence, the footwork.

Once you know that you have taken all of the necessary precautions and are confident that all of your gathered information supports an *educated decision*, it is then time to take that final step and to pull the trigger; it is time to "Fire."

While it may sound simple, sometimes people take these steps in the wrong order or they get hung up on a step, putting their business ventures in jeopardy. At the beginning of my entrepreneurial career, I admit my initial instinct was to spend very little time in the Ready stage and then jump straight to the Fire stage. I thought that I could worry about aiming as I went along. Some people perpetually Aim and never get to Fire. Other people Fire with no preparation whatsoever, and still others never feel secure enough to move past the Ready stage.

Making decisions in the wrong order is a recipe that either creates inactivity and stagnation, or leads to chaos.

Ready...Aim...Fire!

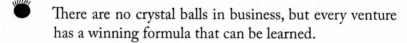

- There are no crystal balls in business, but every venture has a winning formula that can be learned.

- Getting Ready means identifying what you're looking for and getting prepared to take action when the right opportunity presents itself.

- Taking Aim is about due diligence and gathering the information you need to decide which targets are worth shooting for.

- The Fire step happens only after getting ready and taking careful aim—then it's time to pull the trigger!

Sixteen: READY

"It's better to be prepared for an opportunity and not have one, than to have an opportunity and not be prepared."

~ *Whitney Young, Jr.*

Now that you have made the decision to make a change in your life, to take control of your financial destiny, and to free yourself from the pain of obligations, you are now prepared to start working your way across the rest of the river to ONO. You have entered the "Ready" stage of the process.

Being ready begins with establishing a mindset. First, you must want to create change. Where you are now is not where you want to be, but you have figured out what your ideal place looks like. You have a mental picture of your own personal delicious place called ONO.

Second, it may have been necessary to change the way you think about entrepreneurism and making money, and you have done that. Now it is time to take a third step and move from a thinking mindset to an action mindset.

You have already completed the mental, attitudinal steps. You have the keys, and you have the knowledge and ability to create success. You know how to think like an entrepreneur, now you are ready for action. You have to be ready. Ready is being aware of and available to the opportunities that present themselves to you. Ready is having your radar up. You are on the lookout; you are in the process of searching for a venture opportunity that fits your needs and lifestyle and allows you to create success.

A venture opportunity is like a car. The combination of your acquired knowledge and ability is the key to success. Now, literally think of this combination as the ignition key to your car, your investment vehicle. Without the key, there is no way to get it started; it is immobile. You have no business even getting into a vehicle without the key in hand. Let's assume you have this key.

There is one more thing you need to be ready. You may have a vehicle in your driveway, and you may have the key in your hand, but you're still not going anywhere if you don't have fuel to put in it. The fuel your vehicle needs is money.

In order to take advantage of an opportunity that presents itself to you, you must have the financial resources available. Money will allow you to take action. This is why it is so important to have an *established and growing* ONO account.

Seventeen:
Be Aware and Prepared

"Success always comes when preparation meets opportunity"

~Harry Hartman

With so many investment opportunities available to us all, it is hard to choose which ones will be the best fit for you. You can't sit at your computer, search "investment" or "business venture" on the Internet, and expect to find the opportunity that will work best for you with the next click. There will also be times when you get a hot tip from someone in your network, but just because a person tells you about an opportunity that worked for him or her does not mean it will work for you.

Everyone is different. Remember, the goal for your life is to have options. The same goes for choosing a venture. With so many available opportunities, you do not have to settle for something that does not interest you or does not fit your needs and wants. The best way to find the ideal venture for you is to create some guidelines and a framework. In order to do this, there are some things you need to know about yourself before you move on to the process of finding an entrepreneurial venture.

You're probably thinking, "Of course I know myself. I have lived with myself for my entire life." However, I want to challenge you to do a full self-analysis. There's a good chance you will discover some surprising insights.

Get to Know Yourself

You need to find a venture that allows you to be *you*, something that allows you to think the way you want to think. Do you know what your thinking style is? Are you a *linear thinker* or a *global thinker*?

Linear thinkers prefer a structured approach to thinking and learning. They take it systematically and do not move to a new step until the current step is finished. At the other end of the spectrum are global thinkers. They like to see the big picture. They prefer to bounce around from one piece of information to another and continue doing that until they have fully processed all the information. I am a global thinker, or as my wife sometimes calls it, an ADD thinker. She's the one who manages our family calendar. Otherwise, my son wouldn't get to preschool, we wouldn't celebrate holidays, and we definitely wouldn't ever know what was for dinner.

For a global thinker like me, my worst nightmare is staring at a computer all day long doing bookkeeping. The methodical, painstaking process of bookkeeping gives me a headache just thinking about it. For the linear thinkers however, bookkeeping is great. They enjoy the structured method that accompanies this kind of job. The global thinker needs a venture that allows him or her freedom to jump from task to task. A landscaping business would be a great venture for global thinkers. They can mentally see the big picture and they have the choice of which task they want to tackle and when they want to do it.

When you choose a venture, along with choosing one that incorporates your thinking style, you also want to be able to choose one that allows you to work the way you want to work. Some of us are "hands on" workers who like to be right in the mix of things all the time. Those people like to see the result of their hard work. Buying, fixing up, and selling homes could be a great venture for a person with that working style. On the other hand, there are people who feel much more comfortable sitting at their desks in front of a computer. Playing the stock market, day trading, or something along those lines, would be a much better option for those people. Your venture will only succeed if you feel comfortable doing what you do.

Identify Your Limitations

The self-evaluation process does not stop once you have your thinking style and working style determined. The next step can be more difficult. You need to determine and understand what your physical, mental, and emotional limitations are, and how they can affect you in business. GI Joe used to say, "Knowing is half the battle." When you know your limitations, you have the opportunity to address them, figure out how to manage them, and if possible, to eliminate them.

The most obvious limitations are physical limitations. If you struggle with lifting and heavy work, you probably should stay away from anything that is physically demanding. Most people are already well aware of their physical limitations and usually will not pursue something that involves physical demands they can't meet.

However, physical limitations do not necessarily have to become handicaps to you. Many people use their limitations as excuses for not being productive. They spend all of their time doubting themselves and focusing on what they can't do instead of finding something that they are able to do, or on discovering ways to overcome their limitations.

Some of us have genetic limiting factors. As I've mentioned before, I have a learning disability. I struggle with writing and comprehending words and numbers, especially in the correct order. I also have trouble keeping thoughts organized in my head. My disorder is so severe that I was allowed to take college entrance exams orally. It has caused me a lot of grief, but I have learned to use it as a motivation factor. I told myself early on that there was nothing I couldn't do. I created systems that allowed me to break down information so that I could truly comprehend it.

The most serious limitations we all struggle with are emotional limitations. Some are relatively straightforward. For example, if you have a paralyzing fear of speaking in public, then you'll probably want to stay away from pursuing a career in the seminar industry.

Emotional limitations often boil down to each individual person's basic sense of what he or she deserves. So many people struggle with a feeling of unworthiness. This can be disastrous because if you truly believe that you do not deserve success, your failure is guaranteed. Why would someone else have faith in you if you do not even believe in yourself?

Here is the truth: you are as deserving as anyone else of an ONO lifestyle, and you are capable of doing whatever it takes to make that happen.

To battle these feelings, you must be a vigilant assessor of your own mental approach to business, success, and opportunity. I encourage you to be open and honest about your limitations and take the necessary steps to overcome them.

Now here's another little bit of entrepreneurial wisdom: what I have found for myself, as well as for other successful people that I have met, is that *new* limitations show up once you enter into a venture. You will not be able to identify all of your limitations at first. If you are determined to seek out and address every limitation that you could possibly have, then more than likely, you will never get out of the "Aim" mode.

I have learned to make peace with the fact that things will come up that I didn't originally anticipate, and I am open and available to do whatever it takes to move through them. In fact, I look forward to them. They are the wild cards, the tests that make experiences exciting and rich. This way, even surprises aren't surprises, and challenges become just a part of the process. Never stop moving forward.

Overcome Your Limitations

Overcoming your limitations is sometimes hard work, but it is very rewarding and necessary work. One example of personal growth work that many of you can relate to is parenting. There is so much to learn. Having kids *forces* us to work and to grow. The deep-seated duty that I feel toward my two boys was the catalyst for me to overcome some of my own limitations. I decided to bring them into the world, so I owe them my best. I chose to make fatherhood one of the Higher Purpose ambitions of my life. I have received many blessings in return, and have also become a better man.

What's amazing is that this sort of growth is possible in business as well. As with becoming a parent, becoming an entrepreneur, or better yet, a Family First Entrepreneur will force positive changes in you that will help you overcome your limitations. You just have to start. No more toe-in-the-pool stalling. It's time to dive in.

Whether you possess them already or have to work to develop them, it takes two main character traits to overcome your limitations and put yourself in a position of success: the first is a **willingness to grow**, and second is a combination of **will and determination**.

The phrase "willingness to grow" defines itself, but because it is such a big key to the larger picture of success in both business and in life, it deserves further discussion. Everyone has limitations, large and small, and everyone goes through a process to overcome them.

That process involves learning from experience and committing to personal growth. By identifying your limitations, you gain a better understanding of where your weaknesses are and in what areas you need growth. Once identified and acknowledged, the work of change begins and you will move forward. Working toward change might entail counseling, listening to CD's, reading books, watching DVD's, attending seminars, or taking on a mentor who has successfully dealt with a similar limiting issue and learning how he or she did it. Do whatever it takes.

It's About Persistence

We've discussed will and determination before, but I can't stress their importance enough. Without these two personal qualities, your quest for success will be very short-lived. You will start down the path to ONO and at the first sign of a bump in the path, you will probably quit. Will and determination are what keep you moving, and discomfort is often a big part of taking risks. The key is to make the mental and emotional adjustments that allow discomfort to be a part of the picture without stopping your forward movement. This creates a sense of peace as you move through it, and this peace will be like an auxiliary motor that powers your progress, even when times get tough. The most important thing is not giving up.

Many people believe either you're born with determination or you'll never have it. They think that if you were not born with that "I'll never give up" spirit, then you'll never attain it. This is not true at all. Any attitude, including will and determination, can be learned.

The best way I know to experience and develop your own will and determination is to try something. Take an action step. Find something that takes courage and make it happen, no matter what it is. As you move through the action step, a new glow will begin to fill your heart. It's that feeling of; "I am going to do this no matter how scared I am."

Action Breeds Confidence

Once you take that first step, the ball begins rolling, and it is your responsibility to keep it rolling. That first step will lead to a second step, and then a third. Before you know it, nothing will stand in your way. You will gain momentum and confidence with each step, and at the same time, you will learn will and determination. The act of doing evolves into the attitude of commitment.

Here is another way to look at it: business is like marriage. We all hear about how difficult marriage is before we get married, but so many people, myself included, did not bargain for how extremely hard it could be. I distinctly remember times where I felt like giving up on my marriage, but I didn't. Sue and I told each other that we were going to make it work no matter what. We were both willing to grow and to understand each other better, and we had the will and determination to make it happen. Our marriage now gets better every day because of our commitment to one another.

That is what will and determination are all about: an undying commitment to success. That same undying commitment is so important in business. If you want something badly enough, and you're willing to take action to get it, nothing can stop you.

Will and determination can overcome just about any limitation. It doesn't matter what you have in terms of God-given gifts, or the lack thereof, all that matters is that you have guts and a desire to grow.

Remember, it just takes action. You have to jump into the pool first and worry about the temperature later.

Move Along

Getting ready to move to that place of ONO is an exciting step. You begin to feel empowered. You know that with the proper planning and lifestyle, you can be in control of your future and you can set your family free from the weight of financial burdens.

With that said, I must issue a warning: **do not let yourself get too comfortable here**. The Ready stage is not where you actually take control. There is no action in Ready; it is just a progressive thought process. Yes, the Ready step is vital to success, but it is only one third of the equation. Being prepared does no good if you can't move on to the next stage. You're about to stretch yourself and move on towards Aim and Fire.

~ *Opportunity for Reflection* ~

*Do something that takes will and determination
in the next 24 hours.*

Possible suggestions:

- *Introduce yourself to and shake hands with random strangers throughout the day.*

- *Call an old business contact that you have neglected.*

- *Make amends with somebody you have wronged.*

- *Write down a 12-month goal list.*

- *Sell something you like but don't need.*

- *Eat only healthy food for one full day.*

- *Resolve a neglected issue with your spouse and do so from a place of love.*

- *Play a game with your child for as long as he or she wants to play it.*

- *Do something you are afraid to do but that you know you need to do.*

Be Aware and Prepared

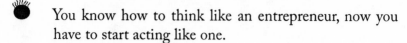 You know how to think like an entrepreneur, now you have to start acting like one.

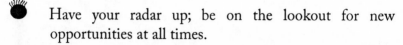 Have your radar up; be on the lookout for new opportunities at all times.

Get to know yourself. Know your thinking style and your working style, and search for opportunities that fit you.

Identify and learn to overcome your limitations.

Don't let yourself get too comfortable in any stage. Forward movement is the key to success.

Eighteen: Actively Create Your Own Wisdom

"Formal education will make you a living;
Self-education will make you a fortune."

~ Jim Rohn

As you move into your entrepreneurial career, the biggest ignorant mistake that you could possibly make would be to assume you have all of the wisdom and knowledge you need to succeed. Why? Because it limits your potential. Remember, moving toward ONO means constantly being in a state of growth, which includes your entire being, not just your bank account. It allows you to take control of your destiny, and makes your potential infinite.

I can't stress enough how important it is for you to constantly be an active participant in creating your own wisdom.

Your brain is like a muscle, and like all the muscles in your body, it will not get into shape unless you work it. Now, if you work your abdominal muscles the right way long enough, you will eventually have a great six-pack to show for it. In the same way, if you work your brain, you will gain wisdom.

Brain exercise can include reading thought-provoking books, attending seminars in arenas that intrigue you, and having deep conversations with people who know more and think differently than you.

Remember, too, "If your lips are flappin' you're not learnin'." In human interaction, the wisest one is often the one listening, not the one speaking.

Keeping the Mental Wheels in Motion

Developing wisdom takes time and concentration and the process works best in an environment free of distractions where you can think clearly. It is so easy to get sidetracked in the course of your busy life. At home, you have family distractions. At work, you have coworkers and deadlines. Even the entrepreneurial world you have constant distractions. You hear, "Try this," "Invest in my product," "Our way is the only way," or "Make millions in no time at all." By making time for wisdom-building, you learn to sift out the valuable information from the clutter, and to adapt the gems to help you reach your goals.

When I need a mental recharging session, I go to the one place where I can rid myself of distractions, keep my thoughts focused, and keep my brain stimulated. I get in my car and hit the road.

The road trips I take by myself provide such an awesome atmosphere for thought. It is some of my only quiet time. I'm away from the kids. I'm away from my wife. I'm away from business dealings, my computer, and with one push of a button, I am also away from my cell phone. What I'm able to do is just sit quietly and think.

The best way for me to get into a brainstorming session is to start by listening to audio information on many different topics. I'll get a CD on foreclosures, and then another on public speaking, and then another on the stock market, or whatever topic I'm interested in at the time. Recordings like these are so much more than new information to me. They are a springboard for my imagination. They provide a catalyst for some very productive and creative thought. In fact, parts of this book were written while driving across the high desert.

We all need to separate from our daily routines, to periodically take a "time out" and be quiet. We need to find places where we can escape and focus, where we can think and get outside the confines and demands of our offices. When you find your place, you will be amazed how much more clearly and productively you think and what good decisions you make. Free yourself to learn, brainstorm, and explore.

Taking on Mentors

My mentors have been invaluable. It's an absolute business necessity to take on mentors who are experienced, knowledgeable, and willing to share their wisdom with you. Mentors will teach you the things you can't learn in high school, college, or from a textbook. They teach you real-world knowledge gained from real-world experience.

To find a mentor, figure out who is excelling in what it is you want to do, and talk to that person. Follow the money and see who is making it. It is best to get advice from people who are not gaining anything financially from you, but are advising you out of generosity. Lastly, it is also a wise move to make sure your mentors are not competitors or potential competitors.

Don't let the fear of rejection or possible embarrassment inhibit you. Don't be afraid to ask for advice. On several occasions, I have approached individuals who seemed to be doing the right things. I wanted to know what made these people successful, so I simply approached them and told them that a mutual acquaintance said great things about them, and then I suggested that we do coffee sometime.

My goal at coffee is to see if there is a possibility of a relationship. I look at whether we seem like-minded in the aspects of business and life that are important to me. I ask myself whether this person could be my friend independent of whom or what they know. If the answer is no, I thank them for their time and keep looking. The possibility of a genuine relationship must be there first, without it, things become phony. If I see it as a possibility, then I move on to finding out how I can add value to the relationship.

Be Willing to Pry

As we get to know one another, I find out what I have to offer them in trade for their time and advice. I am mindful of ways that *I can bring value to relationships;* examples of this might be connecting them to my circle of influence, or even perhaps something as simple as teaching them how to fly-fish.

Each relationship then becomes a give/give situation. To be a success at any aspect of life, it helps to surround yourself with good, prosperous people and to build mutually beneficial relationships with them. **Seek out people who have already proven themselves, become their friend and give them reasons to want to be helpful.**

Remember to use your filters. As you evaluate information gained from a mentor, if something doesn't help you get to your goal, let it go. You cannot take everything a mentor does or tells you as gospel.

Mentors don't necessarily have to be business people. You can learn from just about everyone with whom you interact. You just need to be willing to do the learning, to be ready for it. I've gotten awesome ideas in business and learned many different ways to think from conversations with people who were not even involved in the business being discussed. They can see things from the outside and have a perspective that I don't have.

There is an old saying that illustrates my point pretty well, "When you're up to your ears in alligators, it's hard to remember that your original objective was to drain the swamp." That is how mentors will help you. They've either been in the swamp-draining business before, or they can stand on the bank and give you some objective advice about how to extricate yourself.

Relationships in Business

In addition to seeking out mentors, build your business on a foundation of solid relationships. Being a diversified entrepreneur requires collaboration and support, and the more you expand your business, the more relationships you'll need. Learning how to build relationships is key, so I'm going to walk you through the process by explaining how I do it and with whom. Once again, I want to remind you that the path to that delicious place of Options Not Obligations is different for each of us. This is a "How to Think" book, not a "How to Do It" book. Pay attention to the *reasons* for my actions, not the actions themselves.

Start by building good working relationships with a diversified group of business personalities. I recommend establishing a relationship with a real estate agent, a stockbroker, an accountant, a lawyer, an insurance agent, a car dealer, a general contractor, a banker, a mortgage broker, a financial advisor, and an appraiser. There may be more, depending on what your business interests are.

Some of you may be saying to yourselves, "Why do I need all of these people?" Well, at some point in your life, you and almost everyone else will buy a house and a car and will need insurance.

Also, any entrepreneur who wants to avoid a tax disaster needs an accountant. A good accountant is worth every red cent of his or her fee. My accountant has a personal investment in my success because she knows me well and wants to see me grow. Because of this, she goes the extra mile for me and in the end saves me lots of money.

When it comes to financial advice, a fee-based, not commission-based, financial advisor will help you protect the assets that you build as your ONO account grows. All of these people will eventually need to be in your business family. Keep your receptors up when you meet people who have these skill sets because they can be powerful allies down the road.

Americans waste a great deal of money by conducting transactions with people they can't trust. They get taken advantage of, or they don't have enough information to make wise decisions. To avoid being caught in situations like that, you need solid business relationships.

The first step in establishing a "business family" is to go to people you already know and trust. However, just because you already know them doesn't mean you should automatically enlist them. You still have to do a little research to learn about their business characters, their skills, and their work ethics. They may be very reliable family people and good friends, but their professionalism may be lacking. Find out who some of their clients are and contact those clients to discuss their satisfaction with your potential "family members." **When quality shows up in both someone's personal and professional life, you'll know it's worth developing a serious business relationships with that person.**

While you're bringing business people into your "family," don't forget to consider bringing family members into your business. Being a Family First Entrepreneur gives you a golden opportunity to share the rewards and challenges of entrepreneurism; by letting your loved ones play an active role in the day-to-day work and decision-making.

Referrals

Another way to build your business family is to ask for referrals from the people already in it. Like every good businessperson, your team members will have connections of their own. However, keep in mind that even though this helps shorten the search process, you still need to do some crosschecking before you move forward.

When meeting new and potential business associates, I follow a system that allows me to get a feel for them as people, as well as professionals. I typically meet them for lunch or coffee in a neutral environment. I never start out the conversation by talking business. I begin by finding out as much as I can about each person's life. I talk about family first, being careful not to give opinions of my own. I do this so they will feel free to tell me things about their lives that they might say differently if they knew my opinions and were trying to please me.

I also like to ask them what they do for fun. You will be amazed at how much more comfortable two people will feel around each other when they find out they have common interests and hobbies. Once I have a feel for them as a person, I will then begin to talk business. I just listen as they tell me about their business practices, and then I follow with a question and answer session.

The Honeymoon Speech

The next step in my interview system is, in my opinion, the most important. That step is what I call my "Honeymoon Speech," where I tell that person how I operate in business and what I expect from them. Here's an example of how that speech might go if I were talking with a potential real estate agent.

> As you know, I am shopping for a real estate agent and I have heard some great things about you. In our conversation up to this point, I have established a good feeling about how you handle yourself, both professionally and personally. Jim referred you to me, and he said you are a very trustworthy person. I highly value trustworthiness in my business relationships, and that is what I would like our business interaction to be, a relationship.
>
> I need to be clear about what I bring to the table. First of all, I'm tenaciously loyal to the people with whom I do business. I take pride in bringing all of my business, as well as referral business, to them. I also have solid relationships with a pretty powerful group of people, and if you and I can work well together, I will be happy to share my contacts with you.
>
> I believe that I have a responsibility to you to be a good customer. I will deal with you with respect and fairness. As a giving person, my philosophy is to help those who help me make money, both with referrals and with financial rewards. In return for these things, I expect to be treated fairly and honestly and to get the very best from you at all times. If the trust I am willing to extend to you is ever betrayed, we will no longer do business.
>
> When I enter into a business relationship, I treat it like a marriage, not like a one-night-stand, and I expect you to do the same. The first deal that

we do together will be like our honeymoon. Both of us will be on our best behavior, and you may even do things that you might not normally be willing to do if our relationship weren't new and fresh. I do not want you to do this. I do want you to treat this relationship with the highest respect, but I do not want you taking extra measures this first time so that you can make an impression. I need to be able to rely on you at all times. Show me what I can expect from you from here on.

After our first interaction, I will assess whether we will continue to do business. I'll base that decision on your performance and on how well we work together.

What I have found is that things generally go well after this conversation because I have clearly defined my expectations. Don't make people guess about how you want to be treated, tell them.

Intuition

I also make my decisions about who I work with based on my intuition. If someone rubs me the wrong way at all, I have no problem finding someone new. If I do decide to continue the business relationship, as the trust grows based on solid evidence, I can begin to spend less time and energy making sure that he or she is doing what I need to have done. The result is delicious for me: less time looking over his or her shoulder, more time with my kids.

Unfortunately, my filters are not fail-proof. No matter how careful you are, things can go wrong. Remember, you are dealing with humans. Resolving a troubled business relationship is always tough and learning how to confront people about problems is not easy. This is usually the turning point where a relationship either gains strength or is lost altogether. When you approach a person you're having trouble with, you don't want to come across as angry or on edge. Doing this will automatically put the other person on the defensive and that makes it nearly impossible for either party to be reasonable.

One way to set up the conversation might be to say, "I value our relationship and I want to continue to do business with you but when "X" happened, I knew we had to talk. Now, we could approach the situation from a spirit of defense and attack, but I'd rather we both come from a spirit of humility and learning. My goal here is to find resolution so that we can move on and continue to do business with each other and provide for our families. Can I count on you to have this same mindset as we get into this?"

Taking this approach disarms most people and lets them know what I expect from them. As a bonus, in taking this approach you disarm yourself as well, and set up a safe environment for discussion. It is when a business relationship gets rocky that you will truly know the character of your associates.

Remember, in relationships, intimacy comes after healthy resolution. Healthy resolutions to conflicts are based on honest discussion. If you avoid confrontation altogether, you pass up the possibility of resolution and often build resentment. Resentment will eventually erode relationships. Eroded business relationships will cost you money. Strong vital ones will make you a fortune.

I know it sounds a bit gooey to use words like "intimacy" in business, but that is what I strive for: genuine, long term, intimate business relationships. The network of people I rely on in business would be there for me and my family at a moment's notice, and I would do the same for them. It is a powerful asset to know that you have people like that behind you.

~ *Opportunity for Reflection* ~

*List your potential business family members and
determine the ones you still need to add.*

_____

_____

_____

_____

Actively Create Your Own Wisdom

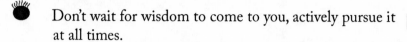 Don't wait for wisdom to come to you, actively pursue it at all times.

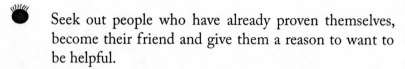 Seek out people who have already proven themselves, become their friend and give them a reason to want to be helpful.

● Mentors are a great source of knowledge. Seek mentors in all aspects of life.

● Successful businesses are built around solid relationships.

Nineteen: AIM

Aiming is exploring the possibilities.

Now you are ready to step into the entrepreneurial world, but which way are you going to go? You have an idea about what you think you would like to do, but how do you get to that point? There are so many different ways to run a business, how do you narrow down your decision? This is where you have to get your hands dirty and begin digging. You have to focus on what will make you successful.

Aiming is doing the due diligence, investigating profitability, finding out if your idea or proposal has the ability to succeed when all the numbers are in place. Aiming is where you make sure that the investment vehicle you are about to step into is actually going to take you in the direction that you want to go. Aiming is the most important element of the Ready, Aim, Fire formula.

Aiming is looking and talking. It's finding out what it takes to make a prospective business go. It's about exploring the possibilities. Buy books on the subject, talk to everyone you can think of that has any kind of knowledge in the industry you are thinking about. Utilize your resources.

Once you have a good idea of what it will take to run the business or investment, the next step is deciding whether this venture is something that will fulfill you. Of course you already realize that you may have to do some things that you don't like to do but which need to be done, such as working nights and weekends, but you still have to ask yourself how you will feel about doing this type of work months or years down the road.

Let's compare the process to Scrabble, my favorite board game.

Twenty: The Scrabble Theory of Business

Scrabble, like business, is about being result-focused.

My mom and I played a lot of Scrabble while I was growing up. She used it as a tool to teach me how to spell. Being a strategic guy, I learned quickly that there is much more to being a good scrabble player than being a good speller. Winning at scrabble is all about strategy. A novice Scrabble player will look at his or her palette of letters, build a word out of those letters, and look for a place to put that word on the board. This style of play will work, but you will never win against a more experienced and strategic player.

Veteran Scrabble players look at their palettes of letters and, before making any words, they study the board in order to find the most advantageous place on the board to put a word that will yield the highest amount of points. They then build a word to fit into that spot. The way to score the most points is to play high point letters on high point spaces on the board. It's about being result-focused. If my goal is to win a game of Scrabble, then I must out-think and out-score my opponents.

Focus on Results

This result-focused strategy can be applied to board games, business, and to almost any facet of life. Most people look at starting a business like this, "I like to shop. I'm going to open a clothing store." This person is like a rookie Scrabble player. He sees a word on his palette, and says, "Oh, man! This word will fit here. Put it on there. Boom! Count it!" He plays the word without considering the number of points it will win him.

By playing that word, has he maximized his potential gain? If the business owner's goal is to spend a lot of time around clothing instead of making a profit efficiently, then that person will probably achieve that goal. But, if he wants to make $100,000 a year, have no employee-related problems, and have time for family and friends, then he should strategize a little.

That means setting goals. Look at what you want out of your business, and then look into opportunities that have the potential to meet these goals. Doing your due diligence is the key. A potential clothing store owner, after researching the industry, will go out and survey all the clothing store owners in the area and find out how much money they make, how much time they spend, and where the problem areas are. By doing this, he can find out whether the business is going to achieve the desired results. That result-minded thinking is the place to start. In order to get what you want out of a business, you need to find a business that can give it to you.

The Four Key Elements

The Scrabble Theory of Business consists of four key elements. They will determine whether a business move is going to be advantageous for you. These four elements are:

- **Time,**
- **Potential reward,**
- **Energy expended**, and
- **Risk.**

Element 1: Time

So what does time look like? Time is the actual physical minutes and hours that you'll be spending on the job. For example, to get the job done well might take two hours, two weeks, or two months.

When speaking of time, however, we also must discuss money. In business, they go hand in hand. As I've told you, I believe that money is time. You trade time for money, so **you must consider how much time a business venture is going to cost.** The operative term here is cost.

When you think of time as it relates to a potential business venture, your goal should always be to make a good investment and to get a good return on that investment. Take into account the cost that you're going to pay by giving time to each investment or business venture. Ask yourself, "From what venture or endeavor would I have to take away time to try this one, and can I afford to do that?"

Often, new ventures are all-consuming at first. Before you enter into a venture, you have to know if you are capable and willing to donate the necessary amount of time it will require.

Most successful entrepreneurs do not have spare hours lying around just waiting to be used up. The time needed to get your venture off the ground will often cut into time spent on other businesses, or time you would normally spend with loved ones. Time is a commodity that can never be recovered once spent. It is the only unrecoverable asset you have, and you only have so much of it in your life. In every decision, ask yourself, "Will the time I spend on this move me closer to ONO?"

To answer this question, we need to give time a monetary value. My goal in business is to keep making my time worth more money with each venture. As my per-hour value goes up, I have more options. For example, let's say that I am a contract painter and I have been hired to paint a house for $1,000 plus supplies. I could paint the entire thing by myself in five days and by doing so, I'd put $1,000 in my pocket.

The other option would be to hire out some help. If I hired one other worker for $300, we could finish the job in half the time. If this were actually me, I would take the second option without question. Why? The answer is in the math.

Example

In scenario number one, I spend 40 hours on the job and profit a total of $1,000. Divide 1,000 by 40 and you can see that I make $25 per hour. In scenario number two, with my hired help, we spend 20 hours on the job. I pay my hired man $15 an hour and it costs me $300 of my $1,000 profit. That leaves me with a $700 gain from the job. Divide 700 by 20 and you can see that I am now worth $35 an hour. At that rate, I can paint two houses in one week, bringing my total profit to $1,400 a week. This is a very simple example, but it illustrates the central point of the entire book: being successful in business is all about *how you think about it*.

Maximizing Earnings

Another way to maximize earnings with minimal time invested is through residual income. Any business that essentially runs itself and produces income falls into this category. Residual income is money earned on a continual basis from work that you have done in the past. Some examples are multilevel marketers, insurance agents, and internet site operators who charge a monthly fee for their services. Let's not forget the king of residual earners, Elvis, whose income is still rolling in long after his death.

Many of these people offer a one-time service to clients but continue to receive income from these clients on a continual basis. Though some people who receive residual income have to do a little follow-up work beyond the initial service, it is one of the best ways to make the most money for the least time invested.

Investments

You may not be ready for this, but I think this is important to discuss. The best way to make money without putting constraints on your time is to have your money making money. If you take this path, it is important to consider the safety of your investments. It is not worth taking a large gamble with your money in order to save time. In order to make this work, you must first have a large ONO account, and second, you must invest your money wisely, in lower-risk and lower-return investments.

To produce cash flow as well as growth through this method, it takes a sizable amount of money. Too many people try to make money this way without accumulating the necessary funds first. They put their underdeveloped ONO accounts at high risk and hope for a break. This has been something that I have struggled with on occasion because I have little patience with low returns. As a result, I learned this one the hard way. I believe that making money (that is, generating cash flow) through investing with a money manager is the final stage of ONO. When you get to this stage, you are financially secure. When done correctly, the time you invest for the income received becomes essentially nothing. This is ONO, and it's very, very delicious.

Element 2: Potential Reward

The next element of the Scrabble Theory is potential reward, or what you stand to gain from your business venture. Remember it is not just about money. Other rewards might be pride, respect, and a sense of accomplishment. But, in a business decision, the first potential reward that needs to be factored into the equation is financial return.

Before you jump into a business venture, it is important to know ahead of time what kind of financial margins are possible. The last thing you want to do is to put all of your time, sweat, and capital into something that you find out isn't going to make money. The first step is to try to get a rough bottom figure and a top figure. I personally prefer businesses with no top. For example, a business with a top would be a hair salon. A single hair salon is limited in terms of what it can produce. However, if you are planning to use your first one as the model for a franchise hair salon, then you have taken off the top. It could be huge.

First, track several businesses that are similar to the one you're considering. Talk to the owners. Find out if they feel spiritually rewarded through their work. Find out how successful that business is financially, and remember, just because that particular business happens to be succeeding or failing, it does not mean that yours will follow suit. Take careful notice of every detail about how the business is operated and estimate the positive and negative effects of each. Evaluate both successful businesses and ones that seem to be struggling. This research will help you calculate a rough top and bottom estimate of the potential financial reward.

> Once you have these prospective figures, be honest with yourself about where you see yourself falling on this scale, and what it will take for you to get there. This is where your work ethic falls into the equation. How much will and determination do you have and how much time are you willing to put into this venture?

Here's how it works. Let's say I meet a woman who owns the most successful business of its kind in the area, netting her $100,000 a year. I notice that the reason behind her success is a combination of great talent and considerable resources. Because I don't have her talent, matching her level of success will mean I have to outwork her. That's something I know I can do. I will go out, beat the brush, and do whatever it takes in order to make the business work.

This is where identifying your work habits, your level of will and determination, and your willingness to grow come into play. When you know how much work it will take to be successful in your potential industry, and you're honest with yourself about your own work habits, you can make good decisions about which ventures will be worth pursuing.

Blue Sky

Another factor to consider when estimating potential reward is what they call the "blue sky" factor. Blue sky is the amount of potential profit a business owner is leaving on the table by not taking full advantage of his or her situation. For example, let's say I'm buying a department store with a large parking lot. The net profit from that venture would be the income from the store, but when I brainstorm about the blue sky potential, I see that I could put a little drive-in coffee stand in the parking lot and either rent it out or run the operation myself. While small additional ventures like this one may not double my profits, they would still bring in additional income.

In some cases, the blue sky profit will be just enough extra benefit to make it feasible to take that next step.

Be Objective

One last thing to remember when you evaluate a business's potential reward is to always make your determinations objectively, not emotionally. Potential financial reward is based on math and calculation. Emotion does not belong in this part of the equation because it will lead you astray. When you really want something, your emotions will tell you that you can do things that you cannot.

Trust statistics. Trust financial figures. If they say no, you say no. It is as simple as that.

Element 3: Energy Expended

We all have four categories of energy: physical energy, mental energy, emotional energy, and spiritual energy. How much of each category is it going to take to get this venture up and running successfully?

1) Physical energy is the actual physical work a person has to perform. Will this venture require you to sit at a desk? Would you have to travel a lot? Are you going to be moving boxes 10% of your day or are you going to be standing on your feet at a cash register? What's the physical expenditure of energy, and is it worth it?

Let's go back to my painting example. Painters constantly breathe noxious chemicals, it is a very messy job, and they perform many repetitive motions. Painters who want to make their time worth the most money work fast and hard. This kind of work is tiring and causes wear and tear on the body. In order to be successful, painters have to expend a lot of physical energy.

2) Next is mental energy. Your brain is a powerful organ, but it can be tiring and maybe monotonous to have to be thinking all the time. How much hard thinking would this job entail? How many hours of your day will you have to spend calculating, analyzing, or figuring things out? Is there constant pressure to make major decisions for the good of your business? As it moves forward, what does the actual day-to-day thinking work look like? This is the pencil-twiddling part

of any business idea. All of these things can really wear on you and erode your ability to function at a top-notch level.

3) Then there is emotional energy. If you are in a business that causes you to deal with the general public day in and day out, that can be emotionally draining. You can also have the emotional energy sucked out of you when dealing with employees. Being in charge of a work force can often be like babysitting. You are responsible for the actions of your employees and the repercussions of their actions. Making sure that employees are on task and are of value to your company can be incredibly taxing on your emotional well-being.

You need to know the nature of the beast before you step into its lair. For example, if you are planning to open a fast food franchise, then you must be prepared for a business that consists mostly of hiring, firing, and training sometimes less-than-dependable employees. While there is profit in this type of industry, you have to know what it is going to cost you emotionally and find ways to deal with and work around each issue, so that you are not drained when you come home to the people you love.

4) The last type of energy, which I feel has the deepest impact, is spiritual energy. It is important here to let you know what my definition of spirituality is. Spirituality is all-encompassing. It is who you are at your core. When I say, "This is my spiritual belief," it doesn't only tie in to what I believe about God, it ties into the spirit that I have within me.

The pure spirit we all have within us is essentially a God-given gift. At times, we mask it with our limitations or our negative choices, such as being greedy rather than generous. Each individual needs to find out how to pull off these layers so that his or her spiritual core can shine forth. I believe an entrepreneur needs to be really clear about spirituality, and really clear about what that spirit looks like. Each person also needs to understand what his or her mask of limitation is and how much it is actually hiding. Once this is determined, we can take the necessary steps to discard our masks.

Remember that spiritual energy is our core energy. It is linked directly to our moral fiber, our sense of self, and our integrity. When we look at a venture, we need to ask ourselves if it will enhance our spirituality or drain it away.

Running on Empty?

In terms of energy expended, you must understand something. *Money does not regenerate energy.*

We have energy tanks, one for each type of energy. Your goal must be to keep your tanks full in order to maximize your efficiency. If what you're choosing to do in business is draining in some way or another, and believe me, it will be, you need to anticipate this as part of the aiming process and develop ways of refilling your tanks. You can't run on empty. Neither can you believe that the money you receive in return for the energy expended will fill your energy tank, because it never will. Remember Scrooge counting his money? Did it really add value to his life? For a while he thought it did, but we all know how the story ended.

However, even though money *alone* will not replenish your energy level, having money can certainly speed up the refueling process. Receiving money as a reward for your hard work will automatically give you a partial refueling. It can ease your mind and spirit to know that you worked hard and that your family has benefited because of your sacrifice. Having money also frees up opportunities for us to take time off.

Time off is not only a reward, it's a necessity. Never underestimate the value of rest and recovery periods when you're working hard. What I mean by that is, if you are expending massive amounts of physical, mental, emotional, and spiritual energy, in your business life or your personal life, then you need to give yourself a chance to replenish that energy. Every individual has different needs and different ways to recharge his or her energy levels. So find out what refills your energy tank and take the necessary time to refill it and recover for the sake of yourself, your family, and your business.

Addicted to Work

Just as I've encountered people who think that financial reward will refill their energy tanks, I've also met entrepreneurs who think that constant work will do it. Believe me, there are many businesspeople like this. Their work becomes the monkey on their backs. They start choosing work over family, work over loved ones, and work over play and the other important things in life. Chris, a business mentor of mine, said it best when he said, "I'm trying not to be a businessman who happens to be married to the mother of my children."

I often see people, and some of them are friends of mine, who miss out on the real joys of life because the thing that has become their replenishing variable is work, as opposed to the greater things in life. Now, I'm not criticizing the type of person, a doctor for example, who gets a lot of fulfillment from his or her profession, or a teacher or a minister, or the millions in the world who serve others. I would only ask such people to think twice about the decisions they are making when their work causes them to sacrifice friends, family, health, relationships, and what they love to do away from work.

There are also some people who have forgotten what they love to do outside of work. I tell people that I mentor, "You need to find a hobby. You need to find something that you love to do that is just for you; it doesn't matter what it is as long as it is fulfilling. It can be art, woodworking, playing sports, sewing, museum hopping, reading books. It can be anything you enjoy doing." We all have an intrinsic need to get out and play.

In fact, I've found a character trait common to many real go-getter entrepreneurs, the ones who really make it—they have learned to play. They reward themselves for their hard work with a little fun. Many really successful entrepreneurs say, "I like to work hard, but I really like to play hard."

Quality Time

As I matured, I learned that playing does not mean going out and expending every ounce of energy in an attempt to have fun. In my earlier days, I would base my satisfaction of a day fly-fishing on the river by how many hours I spent with my line in the water and by how many fish I caught. I have now learned that I can spend half the time on the river, and catch half as many fish, but feel twice as fulfilled. The key to that is making my playtime quality time.

Quality time is so important. Quality time means doing just what you love to do—for you. It means savoring every minute and enjoying it completely. As you begin to spend some quality time on yourself, you're going to find a personal balance between work and life.

If you want to be a successful entrepreneur in the long run, then you need to learn to spend time on yourself. One thing that is often left out of the success books that I have read is that they don't encourage you to regularly refill your energy tank.

Living Your Dream or Destroying Your Passion?

Be cautious about starting a business to turn your passion into your profession. When considering how much time a business venture will require, it's important not to get swept up in believing that doing something you love means you won't mind all those extra hours. Just because someone loves to cook, doesn't mean he or she will be happy with the grueling schedule of running a restaurant.

When I go fishing in unfamiliar waters, I often hire a guide. I always try to hire a young guide. I want the newest guide, one who is fresh, hardcore, and who has cut his teeth on that river system. I do this because my experience has taught me that most guides who have been in the business for more than a couple years are burned out. All of the fly-fishing guides I've ever met started out very passionate about the sport. They loved fly-fishing. They thought, "Here's a way I can make a living and do what I love." What ends up happening though, is that many of these guys didn't consider the potential time, energy, reward, and risk implications. Nor did they check into the industry by asking around, by interviewing people who were already doing it.

If you ask fly-fishing guides about the business, they will tell you, with a little resentment in their voices, that they have to get up at dawn every single morning throughout the entire season, and they work seven days a week. They're in a boat all day, they row a lot, and if they're on salt flats, they push the boat around with a big, heavy pole. This is hard work and many guides end up with long-term physical problems as a result.

The other thing they'll tell you is that they aren't actually fishing for fun anymore; it is their job. They're there for their clients, and those clients are not always easy to work with.

What often ends up happening is that clients come in, and because they paid money, they feel that they deserve to catch fish. They want the guide to do things that are unreasonable, and their expectations are equally unreasonable. A fish is an inconsistent entity. No one can control when or if it will strike. Still, some people believe that because they laid their money down, it is the guide's responsibility to change the nature of the fish and make sure they catch one.

So, number one, the job is physically demanding. Number two, guides become burned out, emotionally and spiritually, by the people they have to deal with.

It doesn't take long for burnout to happen. When guides start to get depleted, they begin falling apart and can't perform well for their clients. They started out fresh and eager, and within a couple of years, they become exhausted and disgruntled. They didn't consider all the implications going in. This is a very graphic example of energy depletion, and I want you to keep it in mind when you're looking at possible business ventures.

Element 4: Risk

The last element of my Scrabble theory is risk. All three of the previous elements, time, potential reward, and energy expended, play into risk. In every venture, you are going to be putting one or more of these elements at risk. You're also going to be risking your investment capital. The key is to determine what the time, the energy, and the potential reward factors are, how great they are, and whether the venture will be worth the potential risk involved.

Veteran entrepreneurs ask themselves questions like these when considering financial risk:

- Do I have to capitalize this business, and what percentage of the total capital is going to be my obligation?

- What will I potentially receive in return?

- o Percentage of the future profits?

- o Shares in the company?

- o Residual returns?

- o Potentially salable business?

- What is the future return on the money I invest now going to look like?

- Will the money that I have to put towards the venture risk the assets I already have?

  - o Am I putting all my wealth at risk?

  - o Am I putting even five percent of my wealth at risk?

The answers will help you assess what you stand to gain (potential reward) and what you stand to lose (potential risk).

It's also important to consider where the money for your investment is coming from and whether you could afford to lose it. Are you risking potential wealth or are you risking actual wealth? Are you risking money that you currently have? Is it money you have earned, or are you working on the "house's money?" That's a gambler's term for when you are ahead and betting with money you've won, not the money you started with.

My Buffer

In addition to my investment account, I also keep a certain amount of money in the bank as a buffer. Buffer money guarantees that I can meet my financial commitments, which includes the needs of my family. Most of the books I've read tell you to have a three to six month buffer. As I told you before, my lifestyle is a frugal one. No one would be able to guess my net worth from watching my spending habits, but even in light of that, I always have a six-month buffer. That would be my advice to you as well. The risk money is the money that I have beyond that amount, and so I assess it differently.

Every one of the business mentors in my life has strongly encouraged me to *diversify*, not only in the type of investment vehicles I choose, but also in terms of the *amount of risk*. I encourage you to do the same. Choose some investments with low risk, some with medium risk, and some with high risk, BUT always do so in light of your assessment of the potential reward.

~ *Opportunity for Reflection* ~

Rate your risk tolerance on a 1-10 scale.

_____

If you rated your risk number over a seven, you are a gambler.

Remember what they say about gambling—the house always wins.

The Financial Goal Tree

You now know several things to look for when assessing your risk, but how do you know how much risk you should take in each of your entrepreneurial ventures? The answer to this question is different for every individual. Some people are much larger risk takers than others. In the business world, high-risk takers often end up getting burned and suffer major setbacks in their entrepreneurial careers. On the other hand, people who never step out and take a risk can end up going nowhere. Remember, the greatest risk of all is never taking a risk. With that said, I'm going to tell you what I feel is the best strategy for managing risk as you move through the different stages of your entrepreneurial career.

You know by now that the goal of your entrepreneurial career is to reach your financial goal, or as I call it, your "magic number." Once you have determined your magic number, think of the process needed to reach that number like the process involved in climbing a tree. The goal is to get to the top of the tree as fast as possible. This tree has several long, skinny branches coming off both sides. In between the skinny branches are thicker, yet shorter branches. While the goal is to reach the top, there are several ways to approach the climb.

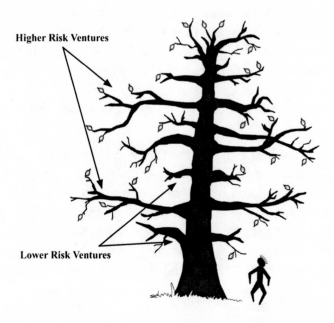

Higher Risk Ventures

Lower Risk Ventures

The first approach is to attempt to shimmy your way up the entire trunk one inch at a time. I compare climbing the trunk to working nine-to-five every day and doing nothing else. You put a little money at a time into a 401K, and wait for the day when you finally have enough money in your account to say you are at the top. Taking this route usually limits the amount of time and available choices you have. Climbing the trunk is a slow and tedious process, and you are usually 60 or 65 before you get to your magic number, if you even get there at all.

The other approach is to climb up the trunk by working your job until you get to the point where the branches start. Each branch signifies a business venture. By the time you get there, you should have enough money in your ONO account to take a shot and go out on your first limb. As you climb, you will see that getting away from the trunk and climbing from limb to limb is a much quicker and more efficient way to the top than inching up the trunk. So, how much are you willing to risk on this venture?

The thickness of each limb represents the amount of risk. The skinnier the limbs are, the more vulnerable they are. You can see that staying on the short, thick limbs or going out on the skinny limbs each have their advantages and disadvantages. The short limbs are much stronger, but you will have to climb three times more of them than you would if you had stayed out on the skinny limbs. The disadvantage of staying on the skinny branches is their lack of sturdiness. There is a much greater chance of the branch breaking, but if they all hold up, it will take far fewer steps to reach your ultimate money goal.

I believe the best route up the tree is to alternate between thick and thin branches at different stages of your climb. In order to get a head start, it is absolutely necessary for you to take a few chances and get out on those skinny limbs early in your entrepreneurial career. Remember, the higher you are, the harder you fall, and during the early stages, you are not that far off the ground. Take the risk and get out where the branches are few and thin. Make yourself vulnerable.

Choose Your Branches

If you go out on a skinny branch that breaks, does that mean you failed? No. As Thomas Edison said, "you just found one way that didn't work." When you hit the ground, you have to pick yourself up, care for your minor scrapes and bruises, and head back up that tree with a learning experience under your belt. On the other hand, if you succeed, you create a learning experience from that as well, and as you grab the next branch, you'll bypass the other climbers who are taking the slower, more conservative approach.

As you get higher in the tree, you have farther to fall. Taking larger risks has the possibility of greater consequences as well as greater rewards. It makes sense to be a lot more conservative with risk as you get higher in the tree. Does this mean that you try to find the most conservative investment vehicle available? Absolutely not. Remember, your goal is still to get to the top as quickly as possible. At the lower limbs, you may have been willing to risk a high percentage of what you had because you had very little. Now that you have a large ONO account built up, you can put a lower percentage of what you have at risk. You have much more to gain if you compare it to the earlier venture, but as far as percentages go, there is much less to lose.

If you continue to make wise business decisions, and you keep climbing, you'll find that the top of the tree is a very comfortable place to be. The view is nice, you have little competition, and the weight of your financial burdens has been lifted. Life is good. You have reached your ultimate goal. You are at ONO.

Play Your Tiles and Get on With the Game

So, in summary, carefully consider the four elements that make up the Scrabble Theory of business: **time, potential reward, energy expended,** and **risk.** Evaluate your findings, make educated decisions, and enter the world of entrepreneurism. It is now time to capitalize on your efforts, play your tiles, count your points, and get on with the game.

Just as I did in the Ready stage, I caution you not to let yourself get too comfortable here—the Aim stage is the easiest place to get hung up. Like Ready, there is no risk involved. It is, however, the last step before risk comes into play, before you Fire. During the Ready and Aim stages, you have prepared yourself for your journey across the river. You can envision yourself in the peaceful place of ONO. Battle that rushing river and move on to your new and better life.

The Scrabble Theory of Business

- Make a habit of asking yourself, "Am I maximizing my potential?"

- Make sure the time and energy you are about to expend is worth the potential reward.

- Keep your energy tanks full; burnout leads to failure.

- Risk is a good thing as long as it is handled strategically.

- Good preparation is the key to great success.

Twenty-One: FIRE!

"Next in importance to having a good aim is to recognize when to pull the trigger."

~David Letterman

Now you have made yourself ready and available for an entrepreneurial venture. You have taken Aim through research and much preparation, and you are at the final stage, *Fire*. The Fire stage is where you put your plan into motion. You have worked the numbers, and this is where your patient due diligence goes from pencil twiddling to action. Your plan goes from an idea to a reality. This is where you earn the title of entrepreneur.

The FIRE stage is the point at which nine out of ten people get stuck. Most people know that their lives are not working, so:

- They gather the information they need to fix them.
- They look across the river and see the people with Options Not Obligations.
- They decide they want to cross the river.
- They test the temperature of the water and scout out some stepping-stones to help them cross.
- They even put their bathing suits on and...

They just stand there. That's right. They get so comfortable making all the preparations to cross, getting Ready and Aiming, that they never Fire. Don't let that be you.

Please don't spend your life like millions of Americans who want something better but never find the courage to go get it.

Dive In. Now is the time for you to step out. You've already tested the water. You've even figured out that this section of the river is fairly shallow, safe, and calm. Don't stand on the shore any longer. Jump in.

Twenty-Two: Logic Vs. Emotion

Emotion doesn't belong in business because it leads us astray.

The Fire stage can be scary. You may feel an abundance of confidence in yourself and in your business plan, but as you start to pull the trigger, that spirit of confidence may shrink and fade. You may begin to think about what you have to lose instead of what you have to gain. You know that once you take action, you're in, and once you're in, you're in. There will be no turning back. You will no longer have just ideas, you will have responsibilities and obligations, and you will have money at risk. You will have put yourself in a position where you are in charge of your own destiny, and that can be very scary for some entrepreneurs, especially in the early stages of their careers.

Have courage. Your first action step, pulling the trigger, will only be scary for you if you let your emotions get in the way of your sense of logic. Basing business decisions on emotion rather than on logic is one of my favorite topics of conversation, especially when I am talking to people just starting out as entrepreneurs.

Spock and McCoy

Think of Dr. McCoy and Mr. Spock from *Star Trek*. These two served on the same ship, the Starship Enterprise, but they had completely opposite personalities and styles of reasoning. McCoy was 100 percent emotion, and because of this, he would have been a horrible businessperson. He would never have been able to make a sound decision because he would let fear, anger, love, or a myriad of other emotions make up his mind for him. Spock, on the other hand, was 100 percent logic and did not allow emotion to dilute his decision-making.

Spock is an ideal model for making decisions in business. Emotion doesn't belong in business because it leads us astray. Unfortunately, none of us is logical 100 percent of the time. We are all human beings, and no matter how hard we try, emotion will always have an effect on decisions we make. We just have to learn to minimize it, especially when fear is making that initial leap tough for us.

So how do you take care of yourself and of your decision to move forward on a project when fear is putting up red flags? The way to overcome those doubts and fears is by using the dispassionate part of your being, the Spock-like part, your logic.

- You have based your decision to move forward on specific, concrete data.

- You have looked at every aspect of your venture.

- You've evaluated your risk factors.

- You've calculated the potential reward, as well as time and energy expenditures.

- To the best of your knowledge, you have all the information you need.

The planets are aligned, and you know that this is a good choice. All the signs point to "**Go**," and because of that, you use logic to regain your sense of confidence, to overcome the pre-fire jitters.

That doesn't mean all the fear will be gone. No matter how hard you try, emotion will still have an effect on you. Fear of the unknown, fear of possible loss, fear of change, fear of acceptance, and fear of doing things beyond our level of comfort are triggered when we consider making a decision that obligates us to move down a new path.

Courage can be defined as doing something in the face of fear. If you don't have fear, you don't need courage. To overcome fear you need courage and, of course, the security that accompanies logic. Then you leap.

My Grandma used to tell me, "Look before you leap." Well, you have looked, and looked, and looked. You've done everything that you could; you've determined to the best of your ability that you have the formula for success. **Now it's time to Fire.**

From Fear to Serenity

Once you make that leap and follow your careful plan, the results are out of your hands. This is where faith comes in, the tool we use in life to operate outside of definable boundaries. I'm not speaking of faith in a strictly spiritual sense. I'm speaking of having faith in your numbers, in your intellect, in your ability to get it done, and in a system that has been proven successful. It's the faith in your work up to this point and the faith in your need to make a change in the status quo. Once you take that leap, let go of the results and have faith that a Higher Power will take care of the results for you.

The fact is that we have no control over the results of our footwork. I may go in with the best business system in the world, the best plan, the best players, and the best financing. That business venture may still go under. That's a reality. There is no way we can guarantee success, because your career as an entrepreneur will have high points and low points. Remember, nine out of ten businesses fail in the first three years. Seven out of ten that do succeed will be operated by someone who has made an unsuccessful attempt at a business venture before.

Does this mean that you have a huge chance of failure on your first venture attempt? Probably not, if you are ready and you take careful aim. You will minimize your chance of failure by doing the proper due diligence. The better the footwork you do, the better your chance of success.

Still, there are many factors outside our control. **Let them go.** I choose to believe that there is a Higher Power who takes care of the details that I can't control. I choose not to worry about these things. Be logical. Be Spock. You and I are responsible for the footwork, the diligence, the action steps that lead to the opportunity to succeed, not for the results. If you don't let go of the results, then you are going to wrap yourself up in stress, fear, and second-guessing. These emotions take energy away as you try to move up the path to your Higher Purpose.

Fire When Ready

Every business venture is a learning experience. If your first attempt succeeds, learn from it and move on. If your first attempt fails, learn from it and move on. It is a natural cycle. If we choose not to learn and move on, we break down that natural cycle. If you never fire, you won't give yourself that chance to learn. Pull the trigger.

It is important for you to create peace with the idea of failure. Every person of wealth has experienced failure several times; many on their first or second venture, but it was their "keep on keepin' on" attitude which enabled them to learn from experience, and to keep going until they reached success. They gained wisdom from their experiences, both positive and negative, and they moved forward and continued their financial growth.

As you move down the path to ONO, you will experience many successes, and a lot of them will be financial ones. As your wealth grows, so will your experience level and your faith in yourself, but, my ONO friend, no growth will happen until you take all three steps, until you **get Ready, take Aim, and....FIRE.**

Still on the Fence?

If you're asking yourself, "Why isn't there more here?" I'm sorry, you're not in the Fire stage yet, you're still in Aim.

Now, if you find yourself sputtering, "I get it. I get everything up to this point, but I need more." You're still in Aim.

Let me say this one more time. If you find yourself here and you think you need more, the place to get more is in the Aim section, and by writing down your Higher Purpose and by making it real. Two factors stop people from firing. One, as I've mentioned before, is fear, and the other is a lack of understanding about how to override that fear.

When you strip down your feelings associated with firing, usually you will arrive at fear. Some of you will be able to overcome this fear with knowledge, that's the reassurance that the Aim step provides for you. If this is you, now you know you need to spend a little more time in Aim and stack knowledge around fear so it doesn't get in your way.

Others know they have all the information they need, and they are still doing nothing. If you are in this category—all the information, but no action—fear is definitely standing in your way. Use courage to create movement.

Overcome emotion with emotion. Use the emotion of your Higher Purpose, which, if you've done it right, should be something so great it can be stacked around fear and dwarf it.

To write this book, I had to push past my learning disability and the fact that I am not a writer. I had to move through some huge fears to move toward one of my Higher Purpose goals, which was to help you and others like you to get to ONO. If I can do it, so can you. Gut check time. Just do it.

Some of you may be surprised to know that before every presentation I give, I am scared to death that I will crash and burn. I've been speaking for years now and that has never changed. I just clip my microphone on and do it. Soon, my passion takes over and my audience energizes me, and I forget all about the stage fright.

If you still want more, you may be the type of person who will stay in the Ready and Aim stages throughout your whole life. The good news is that you now have a chance to break that cycle. Don't give up on yourself; you can do anything you put your mind to.

Logic vs. Emotion

- Think logically; don't let emotion make your decisions for you.

- There will be fear. Overcome that fear with knowledge and confidence.

- Let go of what you can't control; leave the results to your Higher Power.

- If you fail, brush yourself off and try again. Learn from your experiences.

- Fire!

Twenty-Three: Ready, Aim, Fire in Action

ONO philosophy and strategic thought processes can be readily applied to any business venture.

To give you a better idea of how all the stages of the Ready, Aim, Fire approach work together in action, let me walk you through the story of a dramatically successful venture that helped Sue and I begin living out our dream of ONO.

This story involves a real estate investment project, but the important aspects of ONO philosophy and strategic thought processes can be readily applied to any business venture. This is a how-to-think book, so pay close attention to *how* and *why* I made my decisions.

As I discussed earlier, my path to ONO is the story of a series of thoughts, ideas and decisions. I had my magic number in mind as I moved down the entrepreneurial path, but one project put me over the top. It involved the planning, building and selling of a high-end resort home. My wife and I refer to this project as "the President's house" because President Bush and First Lady Laura Bush rented it from us for a week.

Ready: Building Skills and Wisdom

The President's house made the whole concept of ONO a reality for my family, but it was not the result of a stumbled-upon strategy. It was one phase of a meticulous plan that involved Ready, Aim, and Fire as well as the long-term goal to set my family free. As a part of Ready, I had been preparing myself for a project like this for a very long time

I have invested in real estate throughout my entrepreneurial career and have learned how to stage and design both remodels and new homes so they would sell quickly. My first experience dates back to one I did when I was 22 years old.

I made every mistake imaginable on that first project and earned $20,000 for sixteen months of work. Clearly, I had a lot to learn. This is where my "auto-fire" tendency had to be reined in. I had to learn how to be better prepared and take careful Aim before pulling the trigger. I **remained positive** knowing I was learning a wealth-building life skill.

With the knowledge of Ready and Aim on my side, I kept the deals small and used **sweat equity**; I was my own fix-up crew. I also used my venture houses as personal residences for both tax and cash flow purposes.

I bought ugly homes which had the potential for upside profit but which didn't need much capital, just my time and energy. I continued to make my living and did these **projects on the side to build my fortune.** Because I was mindful of making the **maximum amount of money for the least amount of time and energy expended**, I targeted homes that would be easy to fix and produce large returns.

I read constantly on the topic, I talked to hundreds of people and asked them thousands of questions, and I attended seminars to **actively create my own wisdom**. I also sought out several **mentors** who knew more than I did to help me along. I used the **spirit of generosity** to thank these advice givers and actively **brought them value** in exchange.

As I moved from venture to venture, my confidence and my ability to make money on the side grew. By developing this system of creating additional wealth, while not having too much at risk, I got smarter on each deal. I took **lessons learned from previous projects into the next ones**. I became smarter with each project and built a sizeable **ONO account** to be ready for the next one. I kept my eyes open for opportunities and stayed **on the lookout**.

Opportunity Knocks

Shortly before my wife became pregnant with our first son, I heard about an opportunity to invest in some land. It was near a ski resort that was about to be built about two hours north of our hometown. After running national comparisons on what ski-in property was worth, once established, I weighed our risks as opposed to the potential rewards.

I decided to move forward because it was an opportunity to get my wife and me off the road and back to a more stable environment to raise our future family. We wanted more **options** in our lives, and this was a potential solution.

We had a chance to do this deal because we had spent years **increasing our income** and reserves. Because of these efforts, banks were willing to look at us in a project of this size.

Encouraged by what I found out initially, I dove in, crunched the rest of the numbers, and looked closely at the logistics of building an estate house near a resort property literally from the ground up. I began the process of Aim.

As a part of my research and knowing that later I would have a need for a team to help in the project, I began to **build relationships** with the "right" people. By the "right" people, I mean able, experienced, ethical business people. These are people I would be willing to have at my family's dinner table, people who I could trust and consider friends. So, just as Jim Collins advises in one of my favorite books, *Good to Great*, I got the right people on the bus and decided where we were going.

Aim: Hammering Out the Details

When I had a potential team together, I moved further into the aiming process—I decided on a direction. I decided to do the project with little or no cash, which would allow me to keep my reserves in place.

This plan would **lessen the risk** because cash flow and staying power are everything in speculation homes. My theory involved placing my money in ultra safe, liquid accounts to continue to strengthen my family's ONO account while the project ran its course.

I also decided to enjoy the house until it sold, an upside, one of many, to owning a house of this caliber. So, we used it as a "second home" when it wasn't being rented.

Scrabble Theory

Then as the final part of the Aim stage, I ran it through my scrabble theory.

Time – The time was minimal. I had to set everything up, but after that, my time investment was low. I was going to have to give up some profit by hiring everything out, but the margins were there.

- **Potential Reward** – My projections showed we were looking at around a million dollars in profit. I could live with that.

- **Energy Expended** – I love this kind of work. This project was going to give back.

- **Risk** – This project was primarily risking my time and credit report. I had a mortgage strategy that gave me considerable cash to work with. Because of that, my risk on paper wasn't huge, but it was more than I was used to because of the size of the project and the unknown holding time.

The risk was higher than I was used to, but so was the reward. This was my skinny-limb shot at a home run ball. I decided to pull the trigger.

Fire: Making Our Move

The house took a year to sell and my family enjoyed it while it was on the market. We put an aggressive marketing strategy in place and actively worked with our team to get it sold. The stress was high because we had so much at stake. We had to stay upbeat, enjoy the process, and exercise our spiritual resources to **maintain our serenity.**

The project took, in total, about two years and we netted $1,400,000 in profit. My home-run swing sent the ball over the fence, and my family had ONO. In total, my records indicate that I spent 162 hours on this project, and earned $8,641 dollars per hour.

I had a ton of help with the President's house venture and a key player in my success was my builder, Beau Value. Without him, I would never have gotten it done so efficiently, or even done at all, for that matter. He was so helpful. I "**tipped**" him when the house sold. I took him on a moose-hunting trip to Canada. We are still great friends and continue to do business with one another.

In **reflection,** I realize I took on more risk than I realized, but luckily, it turned out well. I learned a massive amount and built solid business relationships because of this project. More importantly, it gave me **ONO** and moved me further along in the pursuit of my **magic number.**

Ready, Aim, Fire in Action

- The ONO principles of Ready, Aim, and Fire can be adapted for any business opportunity.

- Use every venture to learn valuable lessons about how to do even better on the next one.

- Take steps to make sure you'll be ready when opportunity knocks.

- Use the Scrabble Theory of Business to analyze the risks and rewards.

- When all the pieces are in place, make your move and Fire!

Twenty-Four: Reflections

Make peace with learning.
With your failures as well as your accomplishments.

I love evenings. My business day is done. The kids are in bed. It is quiet and peaceful. My wife is following her nighttime routine and taking some time for herself.

I have an evening routine as well. I watch about an hour of one of my favorite TV programs; I record them beforehand so I can go down to the basement and watch one a night. It's the way I unwind. Then I go upstairs. As I walk by Jaken's room, I ask myself, "Have I done everything I could to be there for my little man today?" I reflect on my answer, review my shortcomings as well as my successes, whisper, "I love you, Jaken," and move on down the hall to the master bedroom.

I bend over Tucker's crib, brush his soft cheek with my fingertips and marvel at how peaceful I feel when I'm watching my baby sleep. Then, as I'm doing the mindless tasks of tooth-brushing and clothes changing, I think about my day with Sue, and I ask myself whether I've done everything I could to be there for her. I reflect on my answer, find Sue, and talk with her. I am deeply committed to my marriage and this time with Sue is precious to me. I use it to make amends if I need to, to tell her how much I appreciate her and to let her know how much I love her.

Then I lie down, and, before I grab whatever book I'm currently reading, I think about my business day. As I've done with Jaken and Sue, I review the done, not-done, could-have-done-differently, and need-to-do-tomorrow aspects of my business activities. I do this checkup as quickly as I do the personal ones. I just touch base, and I do it in an easy-on-myself manner.

If I find mistakes, I don't beat myself up about them. I make peace with the rough spots in my business day, and I move on. Shame and regret are best used to move you to action, not to fester or keep you stuck. These evening reflections and the sleep time that follows them help me stay in a place of serenity.

Why do I reflect on the important aspects of my day? Because that's what successful people, do. Whether they have one or several plans in motion, they frequently check in with themselves to see how things are going. Successful parents and spouses do it, and so do successful entrepreneurs. These goal-oriented, result-focused men and women use the last waking minutes of their day to get ready for the first waking minutes of their next day.

WARNING!

Now, I want to make something very clear to you at this point. Some entrepreneurs do not move to serenity after they have analyzed the results of their business day. You might find this to be true for yourself when you first start out.

With that said, I need to issue a HUGE WARNING here: If you do not use your reflection time to create a place of peace for yourself (and I'm talking about *all* reflecting time, spiritual, personal and entrepreneurial), you will actually hurt yourself in the long run.

I've met businesspeople—I'm sure you've met them, too—with dark circles under their eyes. They are uneasy, restless, and living on the very edge of their energy supply at all times. They can't seem to get a good night's sleep and can't seem to wake up without help in the morning. In fact, they don't sleep much at all, and when they do, they carry the business day into their dreams. I think it's called, "burning the candle at both ends." Don't go there. It is a place of agitation, not serenity. It takes you off the path to ONO. It's unhealthy, and it's unwise. This is a counterproductive lifestyle for those striving to be Family First Entrepreneurs.

Reflections are all about hindsight; you look back on your day. Look at your business day with acceptance, because it's done, it's over. I tell myself, "Marc, it is what it is." Tomorrow's another day; it's that simple. Put yourself in a learning mode. Learn. Then make peace with all the learning, with your failures as well as your accomplishments. Thank God for the day's lessons. Move on. Go to sleep.

Reflections

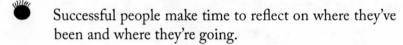 Successful people make time to reflect on where they've been and where they're going.

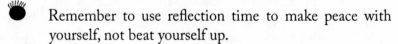 Remember to use reflection time to make peace with yourself, not beat yourself up.

Reflecting and then letting go helps you use the last waking minutes of each day to prepare for the new day ahead.

Twenty-Five: Now What?

Make Your Move

My guess is that you've come to some solid conclusions about what lies down the road for you. Whatever that next step to ONO looks like; I am going to advise you to take it now. **Take that first step.**

Today is a good day to move down your path toward financial security and serenity. Remember, Ready...Aim...Fire!

Take One Step at a Time:

- First: Start an action plan to being eliminating debt (high interest debt first).

- Second: Create a financial surplus by controlling consumption, making more money and adjusting your lifestyle.

- Third: Start investing like an entrepreneur and turn that surplus into your ONO account.

- Fourth: Share the knowledge.

The ONO Journey

Start Smart. Whether this is your first entrepreneurial effort or not, remember to risk wisely. As I told you before, think like Spock. Be objective, not emotional. It is better to spend a lot of time and a little money on your early ventures, rather than the reverse. Your whole

ONO account does not need to go on the line the first time.

Start Small. Remember that many successful businesses were started on the side of nine-to-five job parameters in garages or spare bedrooms: Mail Boxes, Etc. and Blockbuster Video, for example. Keep doing what you're doing nine-to-five and build your fortune in your spare time a little bit at a time at first.

I hope that this book triggers your transition moment and serves as a catalyst for change. A part of my dream, my Higher Purpose in life, is to help people like you get to a place of Options, Not Obligations. If you've made the decision to take your family to ONO, congratulations, I hope this book helps to make the journey easier.

We all know people who are stuck in life. Some live paycheck to paycheck, others are working harder not smarter and families suffer. You can help. Share the knowledge. As a gift to my readers, if you will to go to www.ONOBook.com, and order copies of the book for your friends, colleagues, and loved ones, I will personally sign each copy for you. Enter the code, GIFTOFONO into the promotional box. Live through the spirit of generosity. Share the message of ONO.

Here is the good news: ONO is real. It's not theoretical, and it's not ethereal. In fact, it's like a petroglyph, carved in stone:

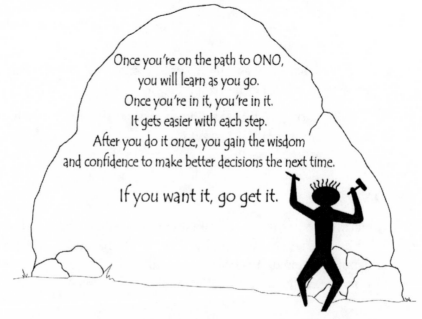

Once you're on the path to ONO,
you will learn as you go.
Once you're in it, you're in it.
It gets easier with each step.
After you do it once, you gain the wisdom
and confidence to make better decisions the next time.

If you want it, go get it.

Bonus Gift
Free Audio Book!

Thank you for your purchase of this book. With it you will receive a free download of the audio version at www.ONOBook.com.

Just go to the site, click on

"Audio Book" and follow the

download directions.

Enjoy!

Continue Your ONO Experience Online

ONOBook.com

- Take advantage of the online resources
- Read blog posts
- Read and submit testimonials
- Plan to attend an ONO Seminar

You can directly communicate with Marc online through his site. He is also very active through online social media:

Twitter: @marcwarnke

Facebook: Marc Warnke

Facebook Group: Family First Entrepreueurs

For information about having Marc speak to your organization or group, please email us at Speaking@MarcWarnke.com.

Marc Warnke's interest in the entrepreneurial world began when he was eight, and by the age 22, he was well on his way to a successful career in business. For the next 15 years he adapted and developed business principles and applied them so successfully that when his first child was nine months old, he was able to semi-retire and become a full-time spouse and parent. He had created the time and money to put his family first.

Marc then decided he wanted to teach others about entrepreneurism and creating work/life balance, so he came out of retirement and *ONO* is the result of that decision. However, as he wrote the book, he discovered that it was really a stepping stone to another higher purpose for him, that of helping bring parents back to their children by helping them become Family First Entrepreneurs as well. Marc trains and speaks on a limited schedule. As he continues his commitment to his wife and his sons, he also helps families and companies learn and apply the principles of ONO.

Marc Warnke, his wife Sue and their two sons Jaken and Tucker live in Boise, Idaho.

BUY A SHARE OF THE FUTURE IN YOUR COMMUNITY

These certificates make great holiday, graduation and birthday gifts that can be personalized with the recipient's name. The cost of one S.H.A.R.E. or one square foot is $54.17. The personalized certificate is suitable for framing and will state the number of shares purchased and the amount of each share, as well as the recipient's name. The home that you participate in "building" will last for many years and will continue to grow in value.

Here is a sample SHARE certificate:

HABITAT FOR HUMANITY

THIS CERTIFIES THAT
YOUR NAME HERE
HAS INVESTED IN A HOME FOR A DESERVING FAMILY

1985-2005
TWENTY YEARS OF BUILDING FUTURES IN OUR
COMMUNITY ONE HOME AT A TIME

1200 SQUARE FOOT HOUSE @ $65,000 = $54.17 PER SQUARE FOOT
This certificate represents a tax deductible donation. It has no cash value.

YES, I WOULD LIKE TO HELP!

I support the work that Habitat for Humanity does and I want to be part of the excitement! As a donor, I will receive periodic updates on your construction activities but, more importantly, I know my gift will help a family in our community realize the dream of homeownership. ***I would like to SHARE in your efforts against substandard housing in my community!*** *(Please print below)*

PLEASE SEND ME _____ SHARES at $54.17 EACH = $ $_____

In Honor Of: _____

Occasion: (Circle One)   HOLIDAY   BIRTHDAY   ANNIVERSARY

      OTHER: _____

Address of Recipient: _____

Gift From: _____ *Donor Address:* _____

Donor Email: _____

I AM ENCLOSING A CHECK FOR $ $_____ PAYABLE TO HABITAT FOR HUMANITY OR PLEASE CHARGE MY VISA OR MASTERCARD *(CIRCLE ONE)*

Card Number _____ Expiration Date: _____

Name as it appears on Credit Card _____ Charge Amount $ _____

Signature _____

Billing Address _____

Telephone # Day _____ Eve _____

PLEASE NOTE: Your contribution is tax-deductible to the fullest extent allowed by law.
Habitat for Humanity • P.O. Box 1443 • Newport News, VA 23601 • 757-596-5553
www.HelpHabitatforHumanity.org

Printed in the United States
143789LV00006B/1/P

9 781600 376016